the Neighborhood Organizer's Handbook

the Neighborhood Organizer's Handbook

Rachelle B. Warren
Donald I. Warren

THE UNIVERSITY OF NOTRE DAME PRESS
Notre Dame   London

Copyright © 1977
University of Notre Dame Press
Notre Dame, Indiana 46556

Second Printing, 1978
Third Printing, 1980
Fourth Printing, 1984

Library of Congress Cataloging in Publication Data

Warren, Rachelle B   1940–
    The neighborhood organizer's handbook.

    Includes bibliographical references.
    1. Community development—United States.
2. Neighborhood.   I. Warren, Donald I., joint
author.   II. Title.
HN90.C6W34   309.2w62w0973   76-640
ISBN 0-268-01447-7
ISBN 0-268-01448-5 pbk.

Manufactured in the United States of America.

To Dianna Michele and Lisa Nicole

Contents

Preface

This book touches on two of the most dominant themes in the value system of American society: the securing of freedom of choice for all persons and the recognition of a pluralistic society. Neighborhoods are capable of being the basic element of human community or a critical link in a larger system of human interaction. The capacity to select and shape one's neighborhood is therefore a key part of the American experience.

Yet there is no single vision of what that neighborhood social world should achieve or represent. Thus, we may consider three traditions of meaning to the neighborhood: the urban village, the frontier homestead, and the ghetto enclave. The first and third of these can be traced directly to European traditions and social forms. In turn, each is related to the major religious groupings of our population.

During the time of the Roman Empire, the colonization and expansion of urban life was linked to an ordered and hierarchical planning of towns using the now-familiar "grid" pattern of streets and roads. The multiple dwelling unit apartments found in large Roman cities can be viewed as the forerunner of the city "block," built upon a single *insula*. This tradition of seeing the most geographically proximate and intimate unit of community as part of an ever-widening set of social levels up to nation-state is part of the Greco-Roman basis of law and philosophy. It is perhaps no accident that the conversion from pagan to Catholic Rome provides a perpetuation of this ordered life expressed in the parish and local neighborhood.

By contrast, the Protestant tradition is one of pronounced ambivalence toward the urban experience. The small rural town with the autonomous "nuclear household" is the most idealized version of neighborhood. People interact not in the central square or piazza but for the special occasions of "quilting bees" or "roof raisings"—neighbors help, but a strong emphasis on the privacy and independence of the household forms a major American value. Even the suburbanite, dwelling in crowded, uniform subdivisions, seems to prefer a contemporary version of the home as an isolated "castle."

There is yet a third tradition of the American neighborhood. It is the transplanted version of the European *ausland*—the ethnic ghetto. Its most pervasive expression in American cities is the black ghetto. This is not an entirely authentic community. It is partly artificial: a creation by a dominant cultural group that carves out a designated locale by which social boundaries and caste aspects of society are maintained.

All three of these historic patterns are part of an uneasy alliance—a kind of neighborhood dialectic expressing one of the unresolved dilemmas of American society. The clash and interaction of these elements continues but not always without overt strife—occasionally of a violent type. This interaction is not often overtly perceived—either by government, residents, or students of the urban process. At best it results in a "creative tension." At worst it is a source of urban blight, decay, and social malaise.

Neighborhoods are a myriad phenomenon. No single vision of the present or future will suffice to encompass their reality. The subject is as contemporary as the "neighborhood organization movement" and as traditional as the biblical injunction, "Love thy neighbor."

Acknowledgments

The background for much of the content of this handbook is based upon neighborhood studies conducted in the Detroit metropolitan area under several grants from the University of Michigan and the help of many individuals with whom we have worked. Previous publication of reports on this research is found in Donald I. Warren, *Black Neighborhoods: An Assessment of Community Power* (University of Michigan Press, 1975) and Rachelle and Donald Warren, "Six Kinds of Neighborhoods," *Psychology Today,* June, 1975.

Through its series of supporting grants, the National Institute of Mental Health provided the resources for carrying out the research on which this handbook is based. Both the Postdoctoral Training Grant Program and the Center for the Study of Metropolitan Problems within NIMH are especially to be thanked for their interest in this area of community analysis.

We are also very much in debt to Helen Hershberger and Bonnie Alcumbrak for editorial and manuscript preparation work. The enthusiasm and commitment of Jim Langford to our efforts is deserving of our warmest thanks.

Perhaps the deepest expression of gratitude goes to the many individuals who so kindly gave of their time and thought in responding to our questions and searchings in understanding their neighborhoods. The openness, helpfulness, and interest of people in our efforts is deeply appreciated. We hope this handbook is a way to respond to their generous contributions.

Introduction

This is a research-based literary "walking tour" through the neighborhoods of America's communities—suburban and central city, black and white, affluent and poor. As an inventory of the rich diversity of neighborhood environments, the handbook is built around a working definition of the types of neighborhood one may encounter. A sophisticated taxonomy integrates the most up-to-date sociological research on neighborhoods—systematically incorporating both the ways in which neighborhoods are structured and the ways they perform important functions of their residents.

The reader is guided through a variety of neighborhoods. We then concentrate on different types of leadership, the range of strategies to mobilize others, kinds of activities the "citizen-organizer" should concentrate on, and, finally, which techniques are most effective in given types of neighborhoods.

Beyond this diagnostic and descriptive content, the handbook treats the subjects of leadership and "group process" within neighborhoods—what roles leaders play and how individuals fit into the social milieu of their residential area. By fitting together insights about the forms of citizen action that have been observed and relating these to the most and least effective match of action to resources of a neighborhood, a series of principles emerge—grounded not in abstract theory, but in the experiences of individuals interviewed in a large-scale study. The handbook thus permits the victories as well as the frustrations of active citizens to be evaluated and compared and to be diffused to other neighborhoods and other groups newly formed or yet to come into being.

There is a historical research tradition that we build upon

1

in the handbook growing out of work beginning in the 1920s at the University of Chicago. Adherents of the "Chicago School of Sociology" approach said, "Let's go out and look at neighborhoods rather than sit in the classroom and speculate about them." Students began a new training discipline—going out into neighborhoods and communities, trying to find out what they were like.

Out of that 1920s perspective on Chicago came the basic idea that the very nature of industrial society was systematically breaking down the close ties between people. This was based on reality since people were forced to move, to roam, to find a place, to migrate for a decent job. When they got into a community like Chicago, men and women had to compete with many others who were also trying to make a go of things. That was the free-market battle for survival. The "Chicago School" told us that certain critical events and values were systematically being bred out of our society: personal, warm ties between people, a sense of community, a sense of identity and cooperation with other people. Accordingly, the very creation of cities was thought to be a mechanism to destroy people's capacity to relate to others in a positive, humanistic way.

On the other hand, if the neighborhood is no longer a meaningful unit, perhaps there is something else, something more modern and efficient that has replaced it. In keeping with our cultural mania for replacing outdated commodities, have we found a better way to cope with the fundamental units of society? Perhaps we have replaced the old neighborhood with something more up-to-date. What might this be?

The answer to this question has generally been that the neighborhood as a primary group has been replaced by various formal systems. People now use bureaucracies in much the same manner as they formerly used their neighborhoods.

We hope to give the reader a specific look at the nature of this change. To do this, we first must take a closer look at what we mean by neighborhood. When we see what it is like in all of its different forms, perhaps we will have a little better handle on how worried we should be if, indeed, neighborhoods are changing, how important this is, and what we can do about it.

To begin, we shall look at the neighborhood in terms of its component parts. After examining each part as it contributes to the whole, we shall proceed to examine the unit itself. What's in a neighborhood? Here we are not examining what it means to be a neighbor, but rather the neighborhood as a form of organization. Our discussion here centers around the building blocks, the components, the structure, and the manner in which neighborhoods function.

This handbook probes deeply into three major dimensions of neighborhood process which represent the intellectual and action-oriented underpinnings of neighborhood organization. We begin with a set of guidelines for deciding the critical *characteristics of the problem* or issue that is facing the neighborhood and facing you, the individual, who wants to take action in the neighborhood. Then on to the important differences in the *structure* of neighborhoods: How are they set up? What sorts of social organization characterize your neighborhood? Of equal importance is the *leadership process:* What kinds of leaders are there? What are their styles? What are the ways in which they see their roles and carry out those roles?

The handbook provides a solid framework for gathering data to obtain a useful answer and—perhaps equally important—a systematic approach to the key questions. We hope to provide the tools necessary to decide whether to start up a new neighborhood group or to work within the existing "establishment"; and how to identify the strengths and weaknesses of a neighborhood.

We begin our explorations with people who are themselves the leadership cadre of our urban neighborhoods—looking at their problems, goals, frustrations, successes, and failures—and then we will go on to place the panorama of neighborhood diversity within an analytical framework.

The reader may, we hope, find our discourse as a useful systematic description of neighborhood life in America's urban areas. Or the lessons and benchmarks may be a kind of "neighborhood organizer's recipe book"—the do's and don't's of taking action in your local community.

But action for what? "Neighborhood power" can be looked at in two different ways. For one thing, it can become the way to protect and organize against what is happening elsewhere. Or we can recognize that the neighborhood is the way that the rest of society reaches out to us. In either case, we can see that if the federal government has a desirable program—energy conservation, for example—its success will be significantly limited unless neighborhoods are given the power to act in support of those policies. In effect, this represents a political tradeoff. Without viable neighborhoods, we believe there cannot be a viable democratic society. It may well be that neighborhood consciousness and organization is the single most promising approach to strengthening the fabric of our urbanized society—to rebuilding the personal ties that the "Chicago School" found to be in jeopardy.

A Word on the Research Basis of this Book

Two major studies over a five-year period provide the essential information from which we have developed our analysis of neighborhoods. A total of 4,500 households in fifty-nine different local neighborhoods provide the raw material from which our conclusions have been drawn. In addition, special groups of local officers of community organizations and people identified as "activists" in their neighborhood were interviewed—another 400 persons.

A special word about the "participant observer" part of our research is called for. Here, we developed a special form of what anthropologists use as a major field method, ethnography. As we use the term, "neighborhood ethnography" is a comparative-research technique based on face-to-face interaction and social-network analysis within and outside of the neighborhood setting. This is fully discussed in chapter 8. It involves a training and short two-week immersion in the life of each neighborhood. Throughout the book, quotations from the reports and discussion sessions held with our staff of "neighborhood ethnographers" are used to illustrate major points in the discussion. In addition, chapter 5 uses excerpts from the survey interviews to provide more of the qualitative "feel" of each local area in which we carried out research.

An Initial Caveat to the Reader

The neighborhood you are in may lack all the qualities we shall enumerate in this handbook. Or it may have several of them in combination. If the latter is the case, you may have more than one good opening gambit and a number of useful follow-up tactics. We can't take you completely through the process with our activist "cook book." And if your area just doesn't fit any of our types, why not just go ahead and carve out a new variety? In any event, we wish you well in the "neighborhood game."

By the way, if you have some success, let us know. We are always in the market for a better understanding of neighborhoods. Don't misunderstand—we think one conclusion a potential activist may reach, using our analysis, is that it is simply not worthwhile to try to work through a neighborhood frame of reference. So we are not advocating an across-the-board "local-control" philosophy as a panacea for the ills of urban life.

But variability of neighborhoods needs to be the basis of any effective social planning and public policy. For the past mistakes of federal, state, and local governments—and the errors of indigenous grass-roots leaders as well—can often be ascribed to an inadequate "seat-of-the-pants (or skirt)" road map. We have tried to improve the road signs and also to show how rich is the landscape of our neighborhood social worlds.

Better is the neighbor that is near than a brother far off.

Proverbs 27:10

A sense of neighborhood haunts our history and our fondest memories.... Neighborhoods can be seen as simply neighborhoods of sentiment.... Cynics say they are never neighborhoods in which people actually live. They are memories; and that's all.

David Morris and Karl Hess,
Neighborhood Power (Boston: Beacon Press 1975), p. 1

1 | What's in a Neighborhood?

In the second session of the ninety-fourth Congress, our government gave official recognition to the proposition that neighborhoods are a national resource.[1] This somewhat belated action has come after a decade in which blacks, white ethnics, suburbanites, inner-city residents, and others have spoken out (often for very different reasons) for their neighborhoods.

The National Neighborhood Policy Act, passed in the fall of 1976, is the first piece of legislative action occurring since the days of the Great Society programs of the mid-1960s that attempts to define the needs of our urban neighborhoods (the Model-Cities Act was the previous one). In an almost rhythmic cycle of a decade, the neighborhood appears and disappears as the cornerstone of citizenship and community in American society. Yet there is a paradox.

As we celebrate the importance of neighborhoods in one research study or via a specific state or federal action program, so we also ignore it in formulating our energy policies, our school curricula, and even our urban planning designs.

Almost everyone has an intuitive sense that the community of place—the proximate neighborhood setting—is a vital part of growing up, of raising families, of meeting many of the changes and stresses of urban life. And often the neighborhood is the target of blame for crime, conformity, and corrosion in the quality of American life.

Can neighborhoods be simultaneously the intersecting point for all of these contradictory trends and social problems? How do we as individuals experience our neighborhood? What are the characteristics of strong and weak neighborhoods? Perhaps these important questions rest upon still another even more fundamental query: What are the ingredients that go into creating the diversity of our urban neighborhoods?

Neighboring versus Neighborhood

A very natural approach to the question of "What is a neighborhood?" is to focus on the eyeball-to-eyeball level—the role of neighbor. Suzanne Keller has explored the idea of neighboring perhaps more fully than any other researcher. She points out that what a good neighbor is depends a great deal upon the perceptions and social norms of people. A good neighbor is not necessarily the good Samaritan who comes over to be friendly and is very sociable. Instead, a good neighbor may be a person who simply minds her or his own business.[2] Keller also distinguishes neighboring from close friendship: a good neighbor is not usually as close as a good friend. If you become good friends with your neighbor, the friendship relation usurps the neighbor relation—"good neighbors . . . are friendly but not friends."[3] One observer in a neighborhood in which we conducted our research put it this way:

> There is a distinction between neighbors and friends in the neighborhood. People will say, "I have my friend. She lives two blocks up—she's not just my neighbor, she's my friend." There is a high mutual aid with the friends who are your neighbors. Little groups of people in the neighborhood are both friends and neighbors.[4]

But when does a person need a neighbor and not a friend? Here is Keller's answer:

> The neighbor is one whom a person turns to because of proximity not because of intimacy and the resources for dealing with 'real trouble'. Small scale, transitive and emergency problems perhaps—but not therapeutic encounters.
> Essentially, the neighbor is the helper in times of need who is expected to step in when other resources

fail. These needs range from minor routine problems to
major crises, and the help requested may be material or
spiritual. Moreover, the help asked for and given is not
unlimited. It is called forth in situations that spell danger
to a group or community as in times of natural disasters
and unforeseen calamities, or that routinely afflict any
and everyone so that the help you give today you may
ask for tomorrow.[5]

There are rules for neighboring. It is not really as casual
as it appears. But what is the source for such rules? How are
the rules enforced? How do you learn about the proper
neighbor role?

Helena Lopata addresses some of these questions in her
study, *Occupation: Housewife.*[6] She points out that much of the
American culture stresses the "proud isolation" of the
pioneer. The definition of "privacy" is connected with the
geographical separation which characterized many communities before the advent of the automobile. Neighbor contacts in this earlier epoch focused on cooperative work and
public activities of church going and marketing—the rest of
the time families functioned in "splendid independence." By
contrast, the waves of immigrants who arrived in the latter
part of the nineteenth and early twentieth centuries came
from European peasant societies where village interaction is
fostered by the close proximity of dwellings to which people
returned after a day's work in the nearby fields. Central meeting places—piazzas, streetcorners, and squares—brought
people into intimate, face-to-face exchanges on a daily or less
frequently repeated routine of contacts.

Taken in its broadest context, neighboring is defined by
regional, social class, ethnic, and other cultural traditions,
many of which persist in some form in American communities. But it is this unpredictable character of the role of
neighbor which is the most basic contemporary reality. Many
different norms of being a good neighbor exist, and they tend
to reflect the shifting role expectations which abound in our
society in such areas as sex, status, and lifestyle. To the question "How can I be a good neighbor?" the answer varies from

neighborhood to neighborhood—or even within the same neighborhood.

Persons who want to organize a neighborhood may be able to do so without jeopardizing their role of "good neighbor." But they must also be prepared to face criticism from those whose notion of "good neighbor" is not oriented toward active involvement.

For our purposes it is more important to ask not what makes a good neighbor—but instead to ask what makes a good neighborhood. Even if there are many answers to this question, we can at least go beyond strictly subjective attitudes and "role expectations."

Are Neighborhoods "Spaced Out"?

Before we can examine the quality and kinds of neighborhoods, we need to focus on what constitutes a neighborhood. Here again, precision is not altogether possible. Are neighborhoods defined mainly or solely by geographical boundaries? In some studies, high school districts are said to be neighborhoods. In other studies, an acknowledged sub-community such as Greenwich Village is thought of as a neighborhood. One study employs the following working definition of neighborhood in Minneapolis/St. Paul: "A family dwelling unit and the ten-family dwelling units most accessible to it."[7] In a study of Israeli ethnic groups, a "micro-neighborhood" is defined as one composed of three families—the respondent's and those of his two closest neighbors.[8] Another researcher uses this same definition in speaking of a "nuclear neighborhood."[9] Yet another approach sees the problem of the size of the neighborhood unit in terms of four social units: (1) household, (2) neighborhood, (3) local area of residence, and (4) municipality.[10] He then describes each unit as interlinked with distinct social functions.

While all of these are reasonable ways to identify spatially the neighborhood, none is totally adequate. In much of our own work, we have used as a basis in proximity the number of first names a person can recall. This corresponds roughly to the anthropological basis of village size—a population numbering approximately 500 families. Our urban schools have used as a basis of elementary school districts a population of several hundred families—the total population usually hovering between 2,500 and 5,000 persons.

Central to the notion of the elementary school district is the concept of "walking distance" of the child. Such a basis of neighborhood is also selected by Morris and Hess:

> What is the neighborhood? It is a place and it is people. It has no defined size or even scale, although common-sense limits do appear throughout history. The homeliest tests for neighborhood would include the fact that a person can easily walk its boundaries. It is not so large that going from one side to another requires special effort. Its physical size means that it is or can be familiar turf for everyone in it.[11]

The first problem encountered in any effort to synthesize present knowledge about the urban neighborhood is the existence of varied and inconsistent definitions of the term "neighborhood." At times neighborhood defines an area with commonly recognized physical properties. At other times it refers to a set of comparatively intimate and permanent human activities and relationships defined by such terms as "primary group" or "neighborliness." This confounding of spatial and social dimensions has made definition difficult and resulted in confused usage and meaning.[12]

Susanne Keller attributes confusion about what is a neighborhood to the following factors: (1) a neighborhood unit's size is confused with its social closeness, (2) assumptions are made about a neighborhood unit without first separating out the accidental elements that are irrelevant to its essential character, and (3) there is a failure to define the role of "neighborhood" when traditional "natural areas" (i.e., those with homogeneous populations, strong social traditions, and so forth) have broken down because of rapid social change.[13]

The very definition of neighborhood is often grounded in the subjective: that basis of relatedness to the society which is accessible or through which the individual experiences society—often first as a child, then later as a parent, and still later as a retired person. Morris and Hess put it this way:

> When people then say "my neighborhood," it usu-
> ally means they have found a place to live where they feel
> some human sense of belonging, some human sense of
> being *part* of a society, no matter how small, rather than
> just being *in* a society, no matter how large.[14]

And yet there is an obvious objective side to neighborhoods involving factors such as the city services available, the upkeep of houses and alleys, the congestion or openness, the style of housing and the way this influences neighborly exchanges or inhibits them.[15]

Neighborhood is really always a dual concept: an image in the minds of those living there or the way outsiders view the area and, secondly, the resources and physical dimensions that characterize it. The understanding of the functions and the social patterns of neighborhoods—their human potential —must be viewed in this sometimes complex combination of factors.

Neighborhoods Are More than a Collection of Neighbors!

Suppose we look for something in the neighborhood beyond neighboring and beyond real or imagined borders. Is it some intangible "at-home" feeling? Is it a false reality? Or is it an elusive outgrowth of other realities and thus a distraction from real power and social influence?

Are neighborhoods merely fictions that people carry around in their heads? If so, then why not just treat neighborhoods as the sum total of the people who live in them? But what about the person who feels a part of a neighborhood even though he or she lives on the other side of town? This came up in a recent planning effort involving a prestigious neighborhood linked to the central park which lent the area its name. As a citizen group began to contact people about the traffic problem in "Academic Park," they found people calling in to join the effort who lived many blocks from the locale. They were at the periphery, but they liked the idea of being linked to the core neighborhood.

A group—even a neighborhood—is more real than its residents may recognize precisely because society is a set of structures and institutions—patterns of behavior that make sense only because of how they fit into the grand scheme of social life. In this view, the most basic thing to understand is not the individual but the group process and organization.

Let us spell this out more fully. We propose to treat the neighborhood as a kind of social structure. As such, it may take on many forms and functions. This concept boils down to a notion that behavior and attitudes—actions and reactions of individuals—take place within a common framework. There are established social norms, roles, and patterns of acting. These systematic or uniform or recurring ways of thinking and doing are what social scientists mean by "social system" or "social structure."

Merely because people live in the same locale or act in similar ways does not mean that the neighborhood is the binding social force. In some way the collective expression of a neighborhood must emerge before it is really a neighborhood in our use of the concept. It is not merely the sum total of the thoughts and actions of people living together in urban space. Nor is it simply anything or everything that goes on in the common setting of a residential area. Something more must be added: a flavor, a style, a consciousness—whether it is positive or negative.

To some degree, then, we can make a first approximation before we see if there is anything "going on" in the neighborhood. If there are no behaviors, roles, actions, or ideas relating to the neighborhood, then residential proximity doesn't mean much in terms of the individuals living there. Still, each person is, at least in part, a neighborhood actor. That part may be minimal. It may be latent. Or it may be active and dynamic. The question is really one of probability: how likely are people living in a given place to feel or act as neighbors—directly or indirectly? This usually indicates some degree of community.

Is the Neighborhood a Community?

In conducting research for this book, the authors were struck by the frequency with which the ideas of community and neighborhood are separated or combined in people's thinking. For example, in talking with black individuals, "community" is very often synonymous with what whites mean by neighborhood. "In my community" for blacks often refers to the most immediate residential environment. In a previous major study, one of the authors developed the view that ghettoized blacks are "socially compressed in urban space."[16] This means that many times the entire social world of the minority person is confined to a mile or so of "urban turf." No wonder "community" and "neighborhood" merge as the latter takes on many of the functions of a geographically dispersed and variegated urban landscape. For other urban dwellers, however, the two become a small, yet often intense, neighborhood life space.

Often what distinguishes neighborhood and community are political jurisdictions or notions about natural boundaries. The neighborhood itself may contain a series of meaningful units. The "microneighborhood" has been defined as the next-door neighbor, the person in the next apartment, or the most immediate set of adjacent households. It is defined when a mother yells out the window to a group of children playing in the street, "Go play in your own neighborhood!"[17] That notion, in turn, leads us quickly into the notion of the residential block as a neighborhood boundary.

Beyond the residential block begins the walking distance neighborhood. The administrative definition of a walking distance neighborhood is usually the elementary school district. In our own research on neighborhoods, the elementary school district has been utilized because it is a compromise between the notion of the very small "microneighborhood" and larger definitions—such as "the west side," the "black community," "my part of town," and so forth.

There are more than semantics underlying the confusing definitions of "community" versus "non-community." Any urban neighborhood is in some ways merely a geographical plot of land which has no meaning apart from the larger urban context. However, in some other ways the neighborhood does possess unique, identifiable features which distinguish it from other neighborhoods. These unique attributes simply reflect the social fact that urban neighborhoods and the social interactions of the people who live there are not randomly distributed.[18]

The distinction between "neighborhood" and "community" should not be made on the basis of the size or "closeness" of social relations. Many "communities" we belong to are "impersonal"—i.e., large and abstract—and the neighborhood may be no different. Indeed, one study of a low income area makes this point: "It is important to keep distinct the ideas of intimacy and common order. A person cannot be intimate with an entire neighborhood. . . . Neighborhood involvement can never be based on intimacy."[19]

In fact, we think the question of neighborhood as community is an open one—an answer requiring some diagnosing and observing, not merely myth building on ready assumptions.

In many cases, a person's community is no larger than the neighborhood. For some people, the neighborhood and the community are the same thing. Nearly half of the people in the city of Detroit and the metropolitan area whom we asked "what is your neighborhood?" answered that they consider the block, or the people living across the street or upstairs or downstairs, as their neighborhood. Therefore, they are talking about something even smaller than the elementary school district. On the other hand, a third of the people regard their neighborhood as being something larger than a "walking distance" neighborhood.

In some cases a community is larger than the neighborhood. In fact, one kind of community may be composed of different kinds of neighborhoods. When people talk about programs and policies for the Polish community, the black community, or some other community, they often forget that they are really talking about a diverse set of neighborhoods.

That's when we get into trouble because we stereotype the black community, the white community, the Polish community as if it had one single neighborhood and as if a black or white neighborhood is automatically the same way in one setting as in another. The point we want to stress is that there are different kinds of black neighborhoods, different kinds of white neighborhoods, and different kinds of Polish neighborhoods.

We will explore the ways to tell whether your neighborhood is a community. Often the answer is that it has elements of—or potential for being—a significant community. But there is no one type of "ideal" neighborhood, just as there is no one perfect form of community. The differences are real and should not be ignored. Unrealistic expectations about the potential of a neighborhood are only sources of frustration and failure. With good analytic tools, you can decide how much, and what variety of, "community" there is in your neighborhood and go from there. Rather than bemoaning the loss of community or neighborhood, it is more important for the organizer to know what does exist—we hope to provide you with the seismographic or "geiger-counter" instruments for doing just that.

A Measure of Sociability (the Sociability Quotient)

"Neighborhood sociability" embraces the number and kind of neighboring patterns across a whole neighborhood. How often do the people in the neighborhood have face-to-face contact with each other? How many neighbors are in contact with others in this way?

The existence of the "sociability" function between neighbors can be an important source of social belonging for the individual. It also serves to mitigate some of the depersonalizing influences ascribed to the urban environment. But this must clearly be separated from exchanges between neighbors which represent friendship and also from very selective kinds of face-to-face contact based only on ready access in its most narrow sense. It involves the willingness of neighbors to exchange greetings or visits.

"Back-fence" exchanges are the essential ingredients of a neighborhood serving as an arena of sociability.[20] Here, people are willing to take advantage of the opportunity to chat with neighbors. Moreover they are comfortable with such exchanges and are encouraged to chat when the occasion presents itself rather than merely reflecting an air of indifferent aloofness. Here is the way this process is described by one resident we interviewed:

> I was out there trimming the tree, you know. And Manny was out there fertilizing his lawn. First thing you know, he was offering me this saw of his and I was trimming everything in sight. The neighbors across the way saw us and we got to talking about the time Jessie fell off the ladder and Tom [yet another neighbor] drove him to the hospital to have his sprained ankle taped up. But, you know, things are like that around here. You get to talking about one thing and pretty soon we're on each other's porches drinking beer and shootin' the breeze.[21]

Such a willingness to exchange greetings invites the opportunity for further interaction.

Neighborhood as a Center of Interpersonal Influence

Although neighborhoods serve as an important arena of sociability for the individual, they also function as a center of influence, both overt and subtle. Prevailing styles within a neighborhood influence the people living there. The focus of influence may range from the way one decorates a kitchen or yard to methods of child rearing and voting preferences.

The neighborhood can be the center of political attitude change, informal advising, and exchange.[22] What begins as simple home-improvement aid can sometimes result in more far-reaching socialization as witnessed in the following example taken from an interviewer's notes.

> Mrs. Smith had come from a staunchly Republican background. When she moved into the "Historic Dis-

trict" she valued the "geneology" associated with her home but stayed pretty much to herself. According to Mrs. Smith, "I already had two boys but when I had Laura I just wanted more space. But that meant adding a dormer or something. Jim [her husband, an electrical engineer] seems to have started the whole neighborhood thing for us. When the [neighborhood preservation] association saw the contractors' trucks, John, Jake and Ed came over to offer their help in encouraging us to do the building ourselves. It was then we were made aware of the strict code for home improvements here. One offered help in carpentry, another in roofing and heating, another in plumbing and Jim already was eager to do the wiring. So we all began. I love this neighborhood. Seems my whole outlook on life has changed. Don't tell my folks, but for the first time I've even voted for Democratic representatives. That shows you what they've [her new neighbors] gone and done to me."[23]

Through the processes of continuous observation of the behavior of neighbors, the "learning by imitation" occurs. This frequently entails neighborhood peer groups of both adults and children. As one of our ethnographers summed up after looking over her field notes spanning a one-year time difference:

We were particularly interested in the Larkin family because they moved in as we had begun our ethnography. They were so different from the rest of the neighborhood. Not in the way they looked but the way they acted. You have to understand that this neighborhood has a fantastically involved parent group and groups of pre-teens, teens, etc. organized for explicit, mutual aid purposes. Behavior is so damned rational.

When the Larkins moved in we noted in our conversations that there was yelling—child yelling at child, parent at parent and all combinations. Talking with that family (and with their neighbors) this year was a real trip. The kids were all on various teams and the parents had been given parties as new residents and asked to join other groups. They (the parents) declined but other neighbors took it upon themselves to have the Larkins over, to invite them to monthly block clubs. Anyway, you wouldn't recognize this as the same family. The atmosphere actually begins to approach rationality.[25]

Mutual Aid in Neighborhoods

Exchange of help between those living in close proximity in urban areas is another frequent and important function. When the rapid response of neighbors is essential, such aid is usually not available from other sources—either kin or formal organizations.[26] Thus, rescue in disaster is made in 75 percent of all instances by neighbors.[27] This means exchanging goods and services of various kinds. It may be as simple as borrowing the proverbial cup of sugar. Often neighbor exchange is part of an elaborate system. The following field work notes provide examples:

> I really don't socialize with my neighbors much, but you know you can count on them. There is the sense that if something happened, they would be there. One kind of thing is if somebody gets a load of gravel or a load of dirt they are going to put on your yard, everybody will come over and sort of throw in a hand.
>
> Or with a friend, you come home and you just bought some beer but it's hot; you might send a kid down with the hot beer and trade it for some cold beer. Or if you run out of sugar. But it wouldn't be like a regular kind of thing. You would replace the sugar.... Maybe a beer or something, but the exchange may be generalized over a long term.[28]
>
> The lady who talked to me said there was a very definite sort of code associated with borrowing. People had breeched that code, but there was an understanding about what you did and didn't borrow and when you did and didn't borrow. For example, there was a lady who used to borrow shampoo every time she needed to wash her hair. She would go from one neighbor to another and borrow shampoo every two or three days. They got together and said go buy your own shampoo. That is not what borrowing is all about.
>
> If you run out and you don't have time to go get more, then you borrow, but you don't borrow something all the time. That is just completely out of place. She said over time they sort of developed a pretty set idea of what you should do. Money falls into the "shouldn't" because it causes bad feelings. Tools are another story. She said: "I would feel terrible if anybody went out and got a wheelbarrow for one use and I had one.[29]

But there are limitations and "rules" about mutual aid:

> I think there is a hierarchy of problems in that local problems like helping a neighbor get a garden together, or paint the house or repair the roof (or with younger families sharing in babysitting or something like that), those kinds of things are solved among neighborhood people.
>
> Even if you got sick and you needed a ride to the hospital, any neighbor could be called upon to provide that help. But then there is a whole other category which is defined by people in the neighborhood as personal problems—your kid has a drug problem or marital difficulty, or something like that—that's nobody's damn business.[30]

Mutual aid can also include economic exchange. People have skills—ranging from knowledge of auto repair and garage building to baby sitting and landscaping knowledge—and such skills provide the fabric of economic exchange that can go on in a neighborhood.[31] Although not part of the regular economy, such exchange occurs with great frequency. One family member fixes the car of a neighbor down the block. In return, the neighbor contributes his carpentry skill when work begins on the auto mechanic's home. Money need not—indeed usually does not—change hands. Sharing and exchanging various kinds of services are commonplace: house tending when neighbors are gone, helping out a sick neighbor, etc.

The role of the local neighborhood as a center for mutual aid may take the form of a protection against outside intrusions as well as a substitute for external support. Thus, refusing to give out information seen as alien to the values of a local neighborhood provides an important protection for the values of local residents. This point is shown in regard to the refusal to give information to bill collectors in black neighborhoods involved in Detroit rioting.[32]

If there is a sudden disaster, where limited resources are involved and the cost of seeking resources outside the neighborhood is excessive, or where protection from external social institutions alien to the local area is sought, mutual aid plays a significant role for many urban families.

Neighborhood as an Organizational Base

People living in a given locale may be "joiners" of many groups. But a critical question to be asked of any neighborhood is whether it has groups or associations such as block clubs, PTAs, or other local organizations that are "for," used "by," and located in the neighborhood. In this way the neighborhood functions as a political and organizational base.

Neighborhood participation may (1) parallel participation in wider circles of the community, (2) compete with other social units in the community, or (3) link with and facilitate participation in the larger community. Fellin and Litwak, in one study, found that where individuals are trying to raise their social class standing, participation in the local community may serve as a basis for moving up and out of the neighborhood.[33] Other research offers evidence that broader voluntary associations are used to speed the integration of individuals into the local neighborhood.[34]

Neighborhood as a Reference Group

The saying "Home is where the heart is" can often find applicability in the local neighborhood setting. After a few days vacation, crossing a major street delimiting the boundary of "your" neighborhood often elicits the "home at last" feeling. Indeed, this brings out another function: A neighborhood can be a basis of identity, a place to which one feels a degree of commitment. In sociological terminology, we refer to this as a "reference group." The influence exerted by neighbors is often subtle and indirect. In this sense neighborhood is a group "in the mind of the beholder" rather than because of extensive social interaction.

The territorial neighborhood is significant as a social context in part because it tends to be organized around public behaviors. Few really care about deviance that doesn't get expressed in the neighborhood. People care about it when it is seen and when it is observable in their neighborhood. Thus, in contemporary society people can do pretty much what they want outside the neighborhood and no one cares. Since the

neighborhood tends to be focused around visible public behaviors, the failure of a neighbor to cut the grass can be more
serious than a personal problem which is acted out elsewhere.
As one neighborhood observer noted:

> This neighborhood prizes newly painted porches. This is
> done "en masse" by the residents who pride themselves
> on the prim exterior of their homes. That's why the in-
> side of Mrs. S_____'s home came as such a shocker.
> Cobwebs covered a conglomeration of congested furni-
> ture with literally no way to walk a straight path through
> her junk. "I found out long ago," she said, "that as long
> as I went along with their compulsive spring painting,
> they wouldn't bug me.... Sure I get invited to their
> block parties now, but I can't stand the damn things. But
> now they don't bother me and I don't bother them. I like
> it that way."[35]

We can say that individuals may be guided and changed in
their behavior and values as a result of what they understand
to be the "social norms" of their neighbors.

Peter Mann, in his general review of the nature of
neighborhoods, alludes to a theme of "things in common." In
this approach he refers to expectations in a social milieu
"where a person feels that people around him think and act as
he does."

> He (a neighborhood resident) thus has expectations
> of a similar outlook on life amongst his neighbors, par-
> ticularly in so far as life in the neighborhood itself is
> concerned. So if people want to go out from the
> neighborhood to work in other parts of the city, if they
> want to spend their leisure time in the city center, these
> things do not particularly matter *unless* in some way they
> affect the neighborhood.[36]

An impressive number of studies have presented findings which support the role of neighborhood "majority values" in a given setting.[37] One such study deals with the relationship of status level of the neighborhood and delinquency
of boys. Using official records, researchers found that boys
who reside in white-collar areas have a minimal chance of
becoming delinquent whereas children from both wealthy

and poor families are more likely to become delinquent in blue-collar areas.[38] The role of neighborhood in mental illness has been discussed as well.[39] Although not seen as "causing" the illness, the quality of neighborhood life has been linked to the development and exacerbation of the illness.[40]

The social climate of a neighborhood may lead individuals to seek out others in an area whom they think agree with them and, therefore, reinforce attitudes they already hold. Merely believing that a majority of one's neighbors agree with you may have the same effect. This "pluralistic ignorance" may be facilitated by the lack of extensive social interaction which makes the urban neighborhood something less than an intimate primary-group setting.

The Neighborhood as a Status Arena

There is yet another kind of activity that can go on in a neighborhood, even a neighborhood where there is not much communication between neighbors. The way people decorate their houses and yards, the kind of car or cars they own, etc., are ways of expressing status, individuality, and economic achievement. The neighborhood can serve as a status arena where people display symbols of who they are and what they have accomplished. Even the way in which gas lampposts are arranged on a block has special meaning in terms of status.[41]

Neighborhoods may act as a mirror of personal achievement and well-being in two basic ways. First, the neighborhood may screen out definitions of class or status which are valued in the larger society but which have no relevance at the local level. Thus, in one blue-collar neighborhood with little deviation in income or housing style, the overwhelming distinguishing characteristic among families is their ability to work with their hands. Craftsmanship takes on a status element with the highest status accorded that family able to build the most elaborate addition to their home and ranging on down to quilting and jewelry making done in small cliques within alternate homes. In this neighborhood, a lack of desire to create something with the hands can lead to a "persona-non-grata" status. In this instance, the neighborhood serves as a generating source of status claims which may replace those valued by the larger society.[42]

The second and more obvious manner in which the neighborhood may mirror personal achievement is by providing an area within which status claims derived from the larger society are "cashed in" in terms of housing, lifestyle of consumption, or other highly visible definitions of social position. The more elaborate stonework or bricking on the exterior of the home, the more expensive automobile, elaborate fencing—all done in a highly visible manner—suggest that the individual is expressing societal definitions of having "made it" in our society.

As status centers, neighborhoods provide local opinion leaders or status figures who may be sought out or interacted with in order to provide what has been called status "bestowal and appraisal," or borrowed status.[43] By selectively interacting with a few neighbors whose status position is atypical of the general area—such as city council member or chief of police who may happen to live down the block—one may find adequate conferral for statuses otherwise threatened by the local area. This observation suggests that neither the total volume of neighbor contacts nor other measures of social participation offer good indicators for this function of neighborhoods. Selective observability of status symbols and the conferral of status where relevant status peers are present may involve a few neighbor contacts to "cash-in" on such claims.

In Chart 1 we have summarized six major social functions of the neighborhood.

All Functions or No Functions?

Most of the time the typical neighborhood does not perform all of the functions we have discussed. Thus, a given neighborhood may be important in performing one role but insignificant in terms of others. Still other neighborhoods may be pluralistic in their functioning—moderately important in regard to several different functions. Both the variety and intensity of neighborhood functions is important.

Chart 1
The Functions of Neighborhoods

1. *As a Sociability Arena*
   Refers to "informal neighboring," "back-fence" chatting, coffee klatches, and front-porch visiting.

2. *As an Interpersonal Influence Center*
   Refers to neighbors sharing opinions, asking for advice, offering suggestions, and influencing each other's behavior and thoughts about many issues—everything from raising children to getting a new job or voting in the next election.

3. *Mutual Aid*
   Refers to the exchanges of goods and services, such as helping out in an emergency, collecting money for a bereaved family or for graduation or birthdays, watching each other's homes when the neighbor is on vacation, or helping a neighbor build a garage in exchange for his help in fixing your car.

4. *As an Organizational Base*
   Refers to local groups and associations such as block clubs, PTAs, and local branches of larger organizations such as girl scouts and political groups, etc. These local groups can become a power base for people in the neighborhood.

5. *As a Reference Group*
   The idea that a neighborhood is a basis of group identity may be reflected in a name residents use to refer to themselves, in a commitment to stay in the neighborhood, or a pride in the neighborhood.

6. *As a Status Arena*
   Provides a place to show personal achievements and well-being—includes parking the new car in front of the house for all the neighbors to see, or decorating the front lawn with gas lamps, grill work, and birdbaths, etc.

Whether a neighborhood performs all of these functions or only some of them is not due to chance. In our current research, we find that particular kinds of groups in society tend to use the neighborhood differently. Evidence from research in Detroit suggests that in the black community, for example, the neighborhood is on the average much more significant as a social base than it is for whites. This is not to say all black neighborhoods are significant in this way, but on the average what we have found is that a black neighborhood is more likely to take on multiple functions than is a white neighborhood. Another perspective is that low-income people, being restricted in movement and mobility, have to rely on the neighborhood more than do the affluent. Income, ethnicity, and race are all factors which give some indication as to what a neighborhood is "asked to do" for its residents.

Social Networks versus Local Neighborhood

There has been a great deal of social research in the last decade or so which has changed our understanding of how urban communities are held together.[44] Much of the work goes against common sense or traditional ideas about the cohesion and functioning of neighborhoods.

Basically, two facts about the urban social environment have emerged from very different kinds of studies and in very diverse locales. The first idea is that people often relate to others only in a context of problem solving. That is, where and how we fit into a community depends on the kinds of concerns we have—for example, day care versus retirement— and the kinds of resources which we utilize. A major study on searching for jobs shows that being in a close-knit small group of intimate friends may be comforting, but it does not provide new leads on employment. This idea put forth by Mark Granovetter about "loose-knit" ties is a very intriguing one.[45] We can sum it up this way: If you have a variety of occasional friends or occasional contacts with neighbors, this may be more valuable to you at a time of crisis or problem coping than if you rely on a smaller number of intimate friends.

There is a second fact of urban life which has emerged from several recent studies. It is the notion that spatial proximity is not the key to community for many urban dwellers. Particularly the middle-class person may be able to telephone long distance, drive across town, or call on a variety of professional services which have no direct bearing on their neighbors or neighborhood. This fact of "nonspatial social networks," as studied by Barry Wellman and others, has far-reaching implications. For one thing, it suggests that the geographical boundary of the neighborhood is a poor indicator of one's "helping community." It also points out that the same geographic neighborhood is in a competitive "market" position as a "helping community" in comparison to the social networks of work, community associations, and family members living at a distance from one's own home.

The concepts of "loose-knit" ties and "social networks" as the key ways people help each other in urban society point to a need to revise our expectations and ideas about how a local neighborhood functions.[46] First of all, they suggest that in many instances what makes a "strong" community out of the neighborhood is not the help of neighbors as the anchor point but neighbors as a set of referral agents. They are the gatekeepers. Suppose a new program or idea can help with a family problem or get something out of city hall for the neighborhood. One important way to have access to that information is via people in your neighborhood who are linked to others who, in turn, become part of the "helping network" available at your doorstep.[47]

In a very fundamental way, what ties you and your neighborhood together as a meaningful link are the indirect ties you have through your neighbors. Just because people who live near you have valuable information, ideas, and inside knowledge about events outside of the neighborhood doesn't mean you will get to use it. That is where the social structure of the neighborhood comes in. If it's the kind of neighborhood where people share information or where there are opportunities to join together and interact, then whatever the resources your neighbors have can be drawn upon in a time of need and whenever you come together.

Thus a neighborhood may be seen as one of the most critical "gatekeepers" for the resources of the entire city. Often the neighborhood may have many of those resources right at hand. In many other instances you can be linked to those resources *because* of living in a particular neighborhood.

The major point is this: Neighborhoods are changing in their meaning for many, if not most, urban dwellers. We can no longer think only of the self-contained enclave or autonomous world of our residential environment. Instead we have to ask, How does the neighborhood mesh into other social institutions and life style patterns? Just as there is not simply one function of the family, so the neighborhood plays a very different role depending upon its resources, the problems being confronted and the alternatives available. Taken together these make up the contemporary reality of urban area neighborhoods.

Neighborhood Redefined

Let us now return to the question with which we opened this chapter: "What's in a neighborhood?" A comprehensive definition of neighborhood should embody both the reality of "loose-knit" and "close" human relationships. Any definition must be universal and encompass neighborhood in terms of different organizational patterns—the fixed elements and the dynamics as well—of the whole neighborhood context. To be useful, our description must say what goes on, who does it, and how they function. The framework for such a task is the following definition:

A neighborhood context refers to the social organization of a population residing in a geographically proximate locale. This includes not only social bonds between members of the designated population but all bonds that group has to nonneighbors as well.

This "larger-than-geographical-neighborhood" definition has several advantages over more conventional efforts to demarcate neighborhood. First, it permits us to look beyond the geographical boundaries that define the people we call neighbors.[48] It gives us a chance to see what resources and "connections" they have that help them as individuals and can help the neighborhood as a whole. Also the "neighborhood-context" approach communicates a very important idea—that people are affected in a neighborhood by more than their individual actions as neighbors. In turn, the neighborhood into which people enter has a history and an identity—a connection to the rest of the community. Whether a person is aware of this connection or not—whether one enlists the help of others to solve problems or not—all of these individual motivations are located in a specific social environment with special strengths and weaknesses. A person may never have to rely on that context. They may never become aware of it, at least consciously. But they cannot escape being a part of it.

Organizer's Exercises
Chapter 1

STEPS TO EXPLORING YOUR NEIGHBORHOOD CONTEXT

Now that we have started our approach and have a concept of neighborhood, let's proceed to draw some roadmaps and guideposts. First, we start by examining how people use the neighborhood. Start with your "walking distance" perception of the neighborhood. Usually the elementary school district is a pretty good approximation. Make it larger or smaller. Think flexibly—but we must start with more than the neighbors nearby or on the block. But try not to cover the "West Side" or the "South Side" unless you really feel it's all one neighborhood. The "feel" of the neighborhood context must involve what is in the neighborhood in terms of social institutions and then what people do, either with neighbors, to neighbors, or for neighbors.

I. HOW TO SPOT THE REAL SOCIAL BOUNDARIES OF YOUR NEIGHBORHOOD

a. What is the sense of distinct neighborhood identity? (We are not speaking about peoples' ties to the neighborhood—instead whether people have a special name including those not living in the area and the degree to which this name occurs in conversations, such as the _____ subdivision, Pleasant Acres, or nicknames that residents know and use.)

b. What is the extent to which the neighborhood has a physically isolated boundary? (You should indicate, in the four directions, how many are marked by major subdivisions, by differences in housing, by physical barriers, or, in contrast, where there is little differentiation between the end of this neighborhood and the beginning of another. You should include each of the directions and what is true of them.)

c. What are the number and variety of behavior settings that are found in the neighborhood? (Here we are speaking about parks and recreation areas, local stores, or churches, street corners, back fences, any special settings that are liable to bring people together or at least to give them an opportunity to interact outside of the immediate household.)

d. What is the extent of commercial activity in and around the neighborhood? (We are concerned here with the number of stores, the size and location of shopping areas, and any sort of regular commercial activity including people in vehicles such as bread trucks and other services available in the neighborhood.)

e. Does this commercial activity cater to outsiders or are the businesses focused on long-term customers and local tastes?

II. HOW TO SPOT THE SIX MAJOR NEIGHBORHOOD FUNCTIONS

1. Organizational Base
What is the extent of organizational activities occurring within the neighborhood boundaries? (This means meeting places of groups, uses of schools or other public buildings for private gatherings and for additional public meetings such as a bank being used for community groups, etc.)

Organizational activity level *within* neighborhood:

0	1	2	3	4	5	6	7	8	9
None									Much

2. Interaction Arena
Is the neighborhood dense with activity?

Neighborhood activity level:

0	1	2	3	4	5	6	7	8	9
No activity									Dense with activity

3. Reference Group
To what extent is it possible to describe a set of common values, problems, or issues in the neighborhood? (The concern here is with visible posters, window signs, or conversational content that shows there are some special concerns in the minds of many people in the area. This may be related to behavior of children, crime, racial concerns, population, street maintenance, the way government is run, or any set of things that seems to be either very frequently mentioned or mentioned with great intensity.)

To what extent are there distinct local norms? (This means things about the neighborhood, whether attitudes, behaviors or physical characteristics, that set this area apart from others that you might compare it to.)

Distinct/special local normative patterns (compared to rest of city):

0   1   2   3   4   5   6   7   8   9

Not distinctive   Very distinctive

4. Status Arena

To what extent does the neighborhood serve as a status display case? (This means people who have spent a great deal of time decorating the outside of homes and front yards with relatively less elaborate backyard investment, the extent to which the outside versus the inside of the house is stressed for decoration and elaboration, the extent to which people have placed automobiles and other consumer goods in prominent display in the driveway or in a visible location. We also include the extent to which people dress up in front of neighbors but are casual in private, such as whether a person comes to the door and says they are not presentable, etc.)

Displaying status in the neighborhood:

0   1   2   3   4   5   6   7   8   9

Not visible   Visible

5. Advice/Influence Center

What is the extent of interpersonal influence between neighbors? (Here the focus is not on the amount of visiting or number of people but on the content of conversations and interactions. This includes seeking to alter the behavior or attitudes of neighbors toward politics, child rearing, family roles, religion, morals, etc., as well as attempts to give advice or willingness to use the advice of neighbors. This could include things centering on house care, how to grow flowers, how to rear children, how to grow old, or just how to grow. If possible the concern is attempts to change newcomers or people who have different values.)

Interpersonal influence between neighbors:

0   1   2   3   4   5   6   7   8   9

None   Much

6. Mutual Aid

What is the extent of mutual aid? (By mutual aid we mean all of those interactions between people which involve exchanging resources including information which may or may not involve monetary values. The stress is on actual behaviors of exchange, not beliefs about the goodness or badness of sharing—instead what is shared or exchanged and how much of it goes on in the neighborhood.)

Extent of mutual aid in the area:

0   1   2   3   4   5   6   7   8   9

None   Much

The New Machines are machines because they are relatively irresponsible structures of power. That is, each agency shapes important public policies, yet the leadership of each is relatively self-perpetuating and not readily subject to the controls of any higher or lower authority.

Theodore Lowi,
Private Life and Public Order
(New York: Norton, 1968), p.
22.

Neighborhoods ... do not persist merely as fossils, as sentimental areas, or as fortresses of special interest or prejudice. Most persist for the simply practical reasons of making life livable and resolving problems which have remained untouched by the movement toward huge, dehumanized scale in social organization.

David Morris and Karl Hess,
Neighborhood Power
(Boston: Beacon Press, 1975), p.
5.

2 | Why Organize? When to Organize?

The purpose of chapter 2 is to help you explore neighborhood resources and understand some of the critical underlying differences that influence successful action taking. First of all, we introduce a basic idea of the different forms that organizations can take. Then we look at some of the discussion of voluntary associations—block clubs, city groups, PTA—and ask the questions, "How do these organizations respond to problems? What are their advantages and disadvantages?" Finally, we address the whole question of the grass-roots networks of neighborhoods. Why are they important, and how can they be strengthened?

Our basic theme in this chapter is that it is preferable, whenever possible, to use an informal grass-roots-network approach to problems rather than relying on formal, bureaucratic organizations.

Community Control

In its most general form, the demand for community control is a form of neighborhood pressure for greater participation in the political and economic activities of their cities. Nathan Glazer has suggested that the issue of community control is part of a general movement against the increasing bureaucratization and centralization of local government.[1] The demand for community control can be seen, then, as a response to the political modernization of American cities. Community control of urban bureaucracies is offered as a means of making these bureaucracies more responsive to the needs of their clients.

Here is a case in point—a resident in one of our research neighborhoods told us:

> We couldn't get the principal's home phone from anyone. We couldn't get it from the school board, and we couldn't even get it from the PTA president. She said, "I'm not allowed to divulge any phone numbers; I don't want to get into any trouble." The parents' groups don't even have access to the lists of kids that are in their kids' classes. So when the PTA does membership drives, they try and get the information that they need about who is in what classes, but the school won't release that to the PTA. But you would think that all those things would exist before decentralization. What's really happened with decentralization is that they've spread the bureaucratic alienation . . . the idea is that under the centralized board, you might have the feeling that it's way over there, and if I went to a meeting I'd get two minutes—all I could do is maybe ask a question. So then they decentralize the thing, and now you've got your own neighborhood place to go to, and you get the same results![2]

The demand for local control and the idea of returning power to the people in their local community and neighborhoods is certainly not a unique one. But as the chorus of support grows and as the debate continues—sometimes at a visible political level, often "underground" and invisible— there is really more than an ideological argument involved. Nor are the special interests of minorities the exclusive bases for considering local control, decentralization, and related return of power to a local neighborhood.

Bureaucrats are not organized to deal rapidly with problems. It may take twenty years to reshift goals. Unfortunately, the effect of many federal programs is to make neighborhoods into bureaucracies. This is because leaders are appointed by outside agencies. When various services and a long chain of commands are added to a neighborhood structure, it becomes burdened with formal layers of leadership of all kinds. Thus, the neighborhood is made into another slow, unresponsive, unworkable bureaucracy.

Let us provide a specific example from a city on Lake

Erie. In our neighborhood research there, we found one neighborhood undergoing racial change. This was an area that had once been Hungarian. Many young black families lived there as well as a substantial number of non-Hungarian, young white families. By tradition, this neighborhood had certain kinds of organization. For example, a local bar owner was really tied into the Hungarian community. For numbers of the older residents who had moved in twenty-five to thirty years earlier, the bar owner was an important part of the community. A repository of information, he knew where to go to obtain the various kinds of neighborhood services—from house painting to marriage counseling.

During this period of racial change, a new person was elected to Congress. Very liberal, interested in trying to deal with the problem of racial change in neighborhoods, he set up a neighborhood office. Although intended as a "walk-in" office ostensibly to "help neighborhood integration," no one walked in. No one was interested.

The bar owner is still in that neighborhood. Young families come—black and white. They get advice. They get information. This local "expert consultant" still screens people for the neighborhood, trying to make sure that potential residents are interested in home ownership and attendant responsibilities. If so, he will help new residents—black or white—find inexpensive (often free) resources and persons with the expertise to advise and aid in home repair. He is the critical resource helping to make that neighborhood work—not that walk-in office set up by some distant bureaucrat.

The lesson here is that residents of this neighborhood were not overtly trying to achieve racial integration. Seeing themselves as neither trying to solve racial problems nor as advocates for the cause, their purpose was simple: housing values were good, they were able to relate to people, and they wanted a good place to live. Racial diversity was a fact—and potential residents were neither encouraged nor discouraged because of their race. The misspent energies of the congressman's office stemmed from the ill-conceived attempts to organize the neighborhood around its racial composition. Agenda setting by outside agencies cannot succeed without local neighborhood support.

Often the positive programs in the neighborhood must be defended from co-optation by well-meaning outside organizations. By turning it into a bureaucratic program, the agency could destroy beneficial activities based upon the natural capacity of people to develop responses to their own needs. Urban problems are not necessarily solved by bureaucratic techniques. On the other hand, there are times when it is best for bureaucratic organizations to provide resources for the neighborhood residents to draw upon. The basic problem of our urban community is the melding of those necessarily large organizations and the neighborhood structure. Linkages must be provided, but it is essential that one is not allowed to dominate the other. There must be a balance. But the problem is, With so many vested interests at stake, how is such a delicate balance achieved and maintained?

In fact there is a general theory about this "balance idea." Essentially the argument is this: Bureaucracy is only efficient when very specialized knowledge is involved and where large scale operation or service delivery offers real cost savings. There are many important tasks best performed by the unique capabilities and structural features of primary groups and other tasks more efficiently and effectively performed by bureaucratic agencies. For example, in situations where tasks are either relatively simple, or where knowledge of the situation is very complex or highly idiosyncratic, requiring multiple responses in quick succession—the primary group will be more effective than a bureaucracy. Litwak and Meyer call these "nonuniform" tasks. They give the following example:

> There are times where the complexity of the situation, its unpredictability, and the need for great speed, make it difficult, if not impossible, to bring experts or large-scale machinery into play in time to do any good. For instance, in our illustration of a mother pulling a child out of the way of an oncoming car, it is not only the simplicity of the act that is at issue, but the inability to anticipate the crisis. Even if an expert were a little better

trained, the probability of an expert (doctor) being at the proper place as compared to a primary group member (mother) is very low and speed is more important than expertise.[3]

"Uniform tasks," on the other hand, are most suited to solution by bureaucracies. These tasks usually involve recurring events that can be broken into component parts, are solvable by specific roles and, most critically, require expert knowledge and a complex division of labor.

The essence of the "balance theory" is that adequate "insulation" must be provided allowing each system to perform in its optimum manner, yet linking them together in problem-solving situations.

In the Litwak-Meyer synthesis of service-delivery strategies, professionals are seen as the primary source of "expertise." One consequence of this presumption is the emphasis—in efforts to improve social-service delivery—on development of improved "technology," techniques of therapy, detection and treatment, automatic information processing, more efficient bureaucratic structures, and more effective means for organizational control over people.

Litwak and Meyer describe a variety of what are called "linking mechanisms" which are used by professional agencies to coordinate the two different, and at times, antithetical social structures of primary groups and bureaucracies. Through these mechanisms—each appropriate for different tasks and circumstances—an agency seeks to influence the norms of local community and to coordinate with the unique activities and capacities of the primary groups of that "client" population.

Here is an example where the "bureaucracy" of the school works closely with the neighborhood:

> The principal will always call when he needs help; he will call up one of the mothers and say, "How about coming over and giving us a hand? Just let your dishes go for awhile and come on over." He knows the names of all the kids. He goes back into the home all the time. If the kid is sick he'll take him home. If the kid does some-

thing good he'll call the mother and say, "Your kid drew a really nice little picture today," and then the next time he calls to say the child did something wrong, she can't say "well you only tell me about the bad things he does!"[4]

"Linking mechanisms" and their uses are part of the 'balance theory" and are a creative departure from a traditional approach to human social-service programming which looked only at formal organizations isolated from their social environments. No bureaucracy can survive for long without effective ties to that "grass-roots" reality. It is a two-way street: Healthy neighborhood ties permit formal agencies to maximize their effectiveness. "Grass-roots" expertise refers to skills and knowledge based on dealing with problems through direct observation and contact where formal training is either too general or too abstract to apply to the immediate situation.

Keeping Grass-Root Networks Alive Is Not Just a Sentimental Goal

If neighborhoods don't carry their load, individuals and families become overburdened and the "client" load of agencies soars—all of which consumes resources and often leaves everyone dissatisfied, dependent, and demoralized. To avoid overreliance we must appreciate the problems and limitations of "bureaucracy." Note the following exchange between a neighborhood research-observer and a resident of what is known as "Copper Valley" (with a high concentration of resident police) in one major metropolitan center:

> There was one woman who had a set of neighbors she didn't like. She called the police on them. [Why not just go down the block and ring the doorbell of any one of the police officers living around here?] Because they don't in general like to be police. I don't think some off-duty cop would run out unless somebody was coming down the street shooting or something like that, and then they might come out and shoot back.
> In some neighborhoods where there are a lot of

policemen you don't call the police. You go down and tell
someone and it is taken care of informally. It never really
goes through the official channels.[5]

There is another point to keep in mind as well. If we
consistently turn over problems to specialized professionals
and distant bureaucrats, it becomes clear that the individual's
ability to come up with new solutions and to have some degree
of self-reliance is going to be systematically undermined.

What Kinds of Problems Can Grass-Roots Experts Solve?

Let us consider some problems which reflect the need for
grass-roots help from neighbors and some alternatives which
may substitute for that help. We find that in all neighborhoods "keeping an eye on the house when someone is on
vacation" is a common exchange between people. The police
department strongly encourages this as an aid in crime pre-
vention.[6] "Housesitting" has in fact become a very well-
developed kind of special role. One practitioner reports having eighty clients and has in fact "professionalized" by in turn
hiring thirty-five other people as housesitters to provide her
with a significant income.

Pat Hersey's Housesitters Incorporated provides a valuable service but also illustrates what can happen if grass-roots
expertise becomes totally formalized into a business.[7] The
example as a whole shows that when a formal bureaucracy
like the police identifies a way to reduce neighborhood crime
but cannot (and should not) be the agency for carrying out
the preventive action, local neighborhood resource systems
must be called upon. When they are inadequate to the job,
outside help is needed—often this simply adds to the reliance
on formal agencies or overspecialized professionals.

In dealing with the whole question of "grass-roots" expertise, a number of examples come to mind. One such
"classic" debate occurred in the city of Ann Arbor regarding
the preservation of a railroad station having historic interest.
The city had developed guidelines regarding historically val-

uable sites and had set up a commission charged with taking appropriate action to preserve such buildings. The owner of the station—now converted into a popular restaurant—desired to expand his facilities which would lead to modifications in the exterior of the building. The debate that ensued involved the city council, the Historical Preservation Committee, as well as a subcommittee of that entity. In all of this, the fundamental question was, If there are rules suggesting the city should preserve historic buildings, then what are the bases for deciding when the designs for using such sites are aesthetically appropriate? The question which was debated for several weeks was not one in which it was possible to call in an architectural expert, although architectural opinions were obtained. The problem was that there was no way for the city to legislate aesthetic values. The only thing the city could do was to indicate a public interest in the need for preserving historic buildings.

The role of neighborhood grass-roots expertise was very important (at least, in this case) in bringing to the attention of the city ways in which such goals were to be achieved. It was clear that there was no objective expert opinion that could arrive at the most desirable plan.

This is an excellent example, then, of the fact that for many kinds of decisions and problems, the role of legislative action as well as of public commissions is necessarily one which draws upon the advice of citizen's groups. But it is not simply a question of the desirability of having citizen's advice. We have here an instance in which the city might well have attempted to define what is aesthetic and pleasing. However, we know the consequences of formal bureaucratic agencies legislating in these areas. Such organizations with their natural tendencies toward uniformity tend to reduce differentiation between one type of solution and another as well as to delay the arrival of ultimate decisions. The fundamental issue is that in many instances, citizen's groups are in a position to draw upon general guidelines and expertise in the same way as the administrators of programs.

Grass-Roots "Experts" for the Neighborhood

Between the formal professional helper and the lay individual are other people who may have joined together or are thinking about doing so. They do not think of themselves as professionals.

One of the things that becomes clear when we think about citizen-action problems is that some of the approaches and techniques require a great deal of invention or discovery on the part of the organizer. That discovery or invention process is often very much located within a set of networks or support systems by which we have come to describe all the ways in which a community works and provides people with the means to solve their problems, or, perhaps more modestly, to cope with them. What we are trying to do is not so much to invent solutions to problems but to learn how people themselves are inventing and discovering solutions. Thus, one way to look at a community is to see it in terms of different layers or strata of resource systems.

It is very important to understand how these systems work as a critical part of mutual aid in neighborhoods. It is important, for example, to know whether all of these systems are present in a given neighborhood or community. Are some of these systems very highly developed and utilized broadly? Are some of these systems virtually absent? How do these systems work together? How do they link together? How do the professional helping agencies relate to the lay-helping system in meeting the needs of people? What is the total set of resources accessible to an individual? One significant point of access is the web of social networks in which the individual is enmeshed.

Charles Kadushin, in his studies of why people go to psychiatrists, demonstrated the existence of "social circles" or networks of people who, through various ties, were linked to psychotherapists. When a personal problem arose for a member of these circles or networks, these people were inevitably drawn into psychotherapy, irrespective of the "objective" seriousness or nature of the problem. The "choice" of service was based on an individual's "participation" or "membership" in a set of these social networks. Kadushin shows the utility of this kind of analysis by demonstrating that the way members of these social circles decide to enter therapy is different at every stage from the decision of nonmembers. An important by-product of this analysis is the demonstration that influence on a person in making choices about mental-health services is not exerted by single individuals but by "social circles."[8]

In recent years a great deal of literature has appeared analyzing the impact on behavior of the social networks in which individuals are imbedded. Some of the studies have emphasized the ways in which behavior is shaped and contained by one's network, and others have stressed the way in which individuals can manipulate these networks to achieve specific goals. Both facets are related to the character and structure of these "social networks" and can determine who seeks such things as mental-health services and information about the availability and types of such services.

We are not surprised to learn that people find out about new jobs through personal contacts more than any other means. Moreover, the nature of these social networks varies a great deal. One researcher found that people who were in contact with others about new job possibilities were often not bound by close or enduring ties but more by what he calls "loose ties"—that is, occasional contacts close to the time at which the person is facing a need to gain job information and by means of a contact which is outside of their conventional social circle.[9] Here, indeed, we are not speaking of "close ties" but of those which form "chains" of information flow which are sometimes lengthy and indirect and in other instances shorter and more direct (for example, from neighbor to the local pub, to a meeting with a "striper" in a body shop who knows of a job opening).

Building on the notions of Litwak and Meyer about "uniform" and "nonuniform" tasks, we can speak about a somewhat similar dimension of problems defined according to how much they are solvable using a wide variety of locally accessible resources. We speak, of course, about human resources: people in roles who can have effective solutions and good ideas—as sound and useful as highly trained professionals. When would this be most true?

For example, a grass-roots expertise problem would be characterized by: (1) observation and control of many (possibly complex) social relationships and behaviors for which a single (outside) person cannot be practically utilized; (2) the presence of theoretical knowledge, even when highly developed, for only a part of the problem or a particular phase, or (3) limited or no agreement in the general population on the definition of the problem.

"Grass-roots" expertise problems involve the presence of one or more of these elements. Now let us mention several examples of these types of problems where neighborhood "expertise" needs to be mobilized.

Head Start Food Co-op:

For the price of $6.00 per family, Head Start personnel purchase vegetables, fruit, bread, and eggs at the Eastern Market early Thursday morning, and distribute the food to the families Thursday afternoon. Most families pick up their bags at the Head Start building, while deliveries are made to those unable to do so.

The structure of the co-op is quite loose. Aside from Head Start "executives," Mrs. B. and Mr. L., who coordinate the program, volunteers are elicited from the community and Head Start personnel. The volunteers may change from week to week. Thus, aside from Mrs. B. and Mr. L., there are no "regulars" assisting in the distribution and collection of food. Labor is divided somewhat with respect to sex. Men pick up the food at the market, while most of the volunteers, who package and distribute the food, are women. The time required for the task (i.e., during mid-day) would rule out participation by men other than those who are unemployed or retirees.[10]

Welcoming New Residents:

There was a young family talking about moving in and being the only young family on the block. It wasn't clear to them whether you could borrow things or not and whether you were supposed to return things within a couple of hours. There wasn't anything like a welcome wagon or an informal thing where they would come over and meet them. They just kind of meet their neighbors over time in the yard, and so on.

If you're a relative and you move into the area, you have automatic entry, you get introduced around to all the neighbors. But if you're not a relative, it's hard. It wouldn't be very easy unless you were a family member or were more or less recruited.[11]

Some problems have elements of "grass-roots" characteristics and also show approaches to their solution which involve formally organized specialization. If we call these "mixed" problems, we mean that a linkage to a bureaucracy is required to adequately cope with the problem. Here are some examples:

Reducing Police-to-Citizen Pressure:

The Northeast police precinct has the most active civilian volunteer extension force in the city as well as the most active police community relations committee. The Northeast residents feel that the precinct should actually be split, as too much effort must be spent in the unruly southern section and the north is left unprotected. Only two other precincts have a civil patrol and the Northeast's is the largest with 125 members. It is said to prevent about 20% of the petty crimes. Each precinct has a community relations committee to increase communication. The committee in the Northeast precinct selects its board of directors rather than having them appointed by the police chiefs as do the other precincts. Meetings are held monthly in the Shrine Church to support the police and to air complaints. Those who attend are mostly senior citizens and the active members from the local homeowners associations, often retired members of the force and their wives or widows, and sisters. The electing of the board, as well as the holding of meetings off city property, is done to keep the workings of the committee away from city control and responsive to the community.[12]

Increasing Citizen-to-Police Pressure:

Many residents accused the police of being negligent. Several incidents were recalled, in which police assistance was sought to prevent a crime (or apprehend criminals), but they never came or arrived too late to be useful. Mr. D. (president of a block club) stated that he and other block members constantly complained about a suspected "dope house"; yet, the police never attempted to investigate the house. The block was only able to secure police assistance when a friend of Mr. D., who was a high city official, intervened and demanded police action. The house was raided and subsequently closed. Although services have improved somewhat, several residents believe that there is a need for better law enforcement, and have thus formed citizen patrol groups, e.g., the Northwest Community Organization and a male resident have volunteered to assist local residents in forming these patrols, which would simply observe and report suspicious individuals.[13]

Still other problems of the neighborhood are largely issues of getting a specific service or specialized expert resource. These are what we may call "low" grass-roots problems. Here are some examples:

Building Code Enforcement:

It had to do with 18 new apartments that had been going up for two years and bothered people. They cleared that up in July with a council meeting. If you had gone in there two weeks ago, it would have been more intense. People from all over were concerned—from Riverside, and so on. The main concern was the looks of the building and the fact that the builder was allowed to build the building and it was falling apart. They didn't have any insulation in the walls. A little baby lives there, and there's frost inside during the winter. The plumbing doesn't work. People were more upset that this guy had been allowed to build that building than they were about the fact that there were lower class black people there. The people primarily concerned were the people right around the building; they're the ones who organized. So this wasn't the total neighborhood. The neighbors really sympathized with the people living there; the guys got cheated. It was mainly the people around the building, but it concerned the whole neighborhood.[14]

Refuse Collection Improvement:

The irregularity of garbage pickup is a complaint of most residents. Aside from individual efforts, complaints of this nature are usually consolidated into block club action. That is, for example, (neighborhood area) Block Club contacts city officials about faulty service on (street) between (street) and (street). Therefore, any improvement in service usually benefits everyone. Mr. D. indicated that a more recent problem is the cut back in garbage pickup due to the city's financial difficulties. He said that because of this reduction, the block club had to practically "plead" with residents to maintain their garbage in the proper containers until the city would pick them up.[15]

Any problem area may have a "high," "medium," or "low" grass-roots version. Chart 2 elaborates on these three categories and gives some characteristic examples of each.

Particularly, medium and high grass-roots expertise problems may be and can often be handled entirely outside the formal professional and service-delivery systems of the community. Also, they cannot by definition be effectively dealt with as a community solely by the formal organization. Additional informal systems must be developed or utilized by the individual. Also, even where a task has a high degree of visibility and there is legitimate professional expertise associated with its initial labeling or identification, follow-up and maintenance actions are often largely functions of the informal helping systems embodied in local neighborhoods— networks of neighbors, friends, kin, co-workers, and other community institutions. Such problems can range from mental and physical health impairments to building-code violations.

Choice of Problems and the Neighborhood Setting

There are three central reasons for differentiating among problems as we have done in this chapter: (1) the role of primary groups or informal helping systems may vary considerably in determining the coping capacity of the individual and the neighborhood; (2) given kinds of locales or population groups may be more able to provide significant coping resources depending on the type of problem; and (3) the value of professional resources will vary across problem type regardless of the locale.

Chart 2
A Typology of Neighborhood Related Problems Based on the Role of Grass-Roots Expertise

	High Grass-Roots Expertise (Low Professional Expertise)	Medium Grass-Roots Expertise (Medium Professional Expertise)	Low Grass-Roots Expertise (High Professional Expertise)
Newcomers to the Neighborhood	Helping a new family feel more comfortable in the neighborhood	Best way to let new families know about local services	Locating special services for new families
Citizen-Police Organization	Need for citizen patrol to help police	Kind of activities of citizen patrol	Training of police officers in relating to citizen patrols
Use of Police for help	Reasons people don't call on police to help	Police emphasis in patroling, squad-car, and foot-patrol duties	Best use of police car versus foot patrol
Parent School Organization	Best times and places for parents in local PTA to meet	Role of parents in the local PTA	Cost accounting methods for PTA group to use
Traffic Patterns	Need for new curb cuts to include a commercial use	Location of street curb cuts	Monitoring traffic safety patterns associated with curb cuts
Overall Neighborhood planning	Planning goals for the neighborhood	Best contractors to use in implementing planning goals	Best materials to use on home improvement and code enforcement repairs
Police/Family Problems	Whether to call police in local domestic disputes	Behavior or rules of police in handling domestic dispute situations	Best kind of dispatch alarm system to use by police
Recreation Activities	Best way for citizens to use recreation facilities	Reasons for nonuse of community center	Construction materials to use in recreation facilities
Neighborhood Upkeep	Motivating people to stop littering	Deciding on most serious pollution problem	Locating devices to measure air or water pollution
School Crossing Guards	Best people to act as street guards for school children	Number of street crossing guards needed for school children	Type of signs to be used by crossing guards

With the above considerations in mind, our view of the relationship of bureaucracies (agencies) and primary groups (such as the neighborhood) is fundamentally altered. If professionals are treating only a fraction of the people who have problems, if people are coping (often quite adequately) by using informal systems of social support, if the "expertise" given by professionals is seriously affected by confirmation or disconfirmation in one's social network, and if preventative measures are needed, then more must be kept in mind than a desire to take action.

Are there some kinds of values that have not been recognized by the residents but which are found in the kinds of uses they are presently making of their neighborhood? To the extent that there is some consideration of the culture or values of the neighborhood, then to that degree these represent "grass-roots" kinds of decisions (those in which there can be no set rules), and the "complexity" of the problem is closely tied to the needs and desires of the people presently residing in the area.

Thus, the first decision that the neighborhood activist must make is how much of the problem is due to the character of needs, desires, perceptions, kinds of concerns which are not clearly in the "jurisdictional domain" of a given city agency or department? How much of the problem is really a matter of interpreting or enforcing the rules that have been laid down by city hall? Is it a problem, for example, of trying to get people in the neighborhood to be more careful about the way they use that environment? (Therefore, the city ought to be called upon to strengthen regulations, enforce zoning restrictions, enforce sanitary codes and building codes.) Or are these very rules and regulations simply too cumbersome or perhaps too general? Or are they perhaps too restrictive? These are some of the initial judgments which must be made by the neighborhood activist: "What is the nature of the issue?"

One question that must be confronted when we look at our overall discussion is, "When to organize?" This involves examination of the kind of elements that are in dispute with regard to the existing level of knowledge. Some problems are simply a matter of political or ideological argumentation; others seem difficult to define, much less to solve.[16]

Thus, the organizer—or the activist in a neighborhood—must first of all make some diagnosis about the nature of the problem. Is it, for example, a matter of city engineers making an estimate of the traffic load in a neighborhood and indicating that greater restrictions on the flow of traffic are called for? Is this the kind of a problem with which the neighborhood, if organized, is very likely to succeed? Or, if we take another problem such as an effort to redevelop portions of a neighborhood, what are the desirable characteristics of that neighborhood which make it viable? Here, the question may well turn on the values and attitudes of the residents themselves. What do they consider the neighborhood to be most desirable for? What kind of image do they have of their neighborhood? Do they like bustling commercial activity at the fringe? Do they want to be totally a quiet residential area?

Clearly, many of the decisions about what problems to act on from the "grass-roots" level or from the "formal-agency" perspective depend on who is initiating the intervention. Value and goal issues cannot be resolved just by attempting to define the problem at hand more specifically. But the approach taken in this chapter has sought to sharpen and perhaps to permit some selection among the choices open to the neighborhood organizer—amateur or professional, the lone "change agent" or the member of a group or service agency.

Organizer's Exercises
Chapter 2

PROBLEM/ISSUE TYPES: "GRASS-ROOTS" VERSUS FORMAL ACTION

How much "grass-roots" action is required and how much "formal" action is needed? Score each of the following on the "formal action" side versus the "grass-roots" side.

The issue or problem is characterized by: _____

_____

_____

Questions to ask about the organizing task:

1. Is it an issue where very specialized or technical information is involved?

    YES   NO

    Formal   In-Between   Grass roots

2. Is it an issue where there is more than one known approach or solution that you know can be successful?

    YES   NO

    Grass Roots   In-Between   Formal

3. Is it an issue where the problem is so **new that** most people don't even think in terms of the idea?

    YES   NO

    Grass Roots   In-Between   Formal

4. Is there a change in people's attitudes required before effective action is to occur or a solution to be found?

    YES   NO

    Grass Roots   In-Between   Formal

5. Is it a matter of getting people to adopt a special kind of behavior—to *do* something differently—rather than asking them to *think* differently?

    YES   NO

    Formal   In-Between   Grass Roots

6. Does the issue require a single action rather than a series of continuing or follow-up actions?

    YES   NO

    Formal   In-Between   Grass Roots

7. When the problem comes up, does it usually recur in the same way, i.e., has the same pattern or symptoms?

    YES   NO

    Formal   In-Between   Grass Roots

8. When the problem comes up does it take on so many forms and shapes that it is hard to see it as one unified problem?

    YES   NO

    Grass Roots   In-Between   Formal

Now add the YES's for formal action and for "grass roots," assigning two points for each and giving a single point to each side for an "in-between" answer. The final score provides a good description of the type of issue you are dealing with.

There is one factor to keep very much in your mind: "city hall" means more than the specific governmental apparatus. This may indeed be very ineffective, corrupt, or the wrong political persuasion to be receptive to your concerns. It may mean you have to go out and hire some outside group to look at the problem—call in some special set of experts of your own—and then put together some formal structure to deal with the mechanics of carrying out the program you want. A high score on the formal-action side means you have to do this early in the issue and keep on using that structure. A high "grass-roots" score means using formal roles and expertise on certain parts at selected points in the issue's development or in some instances totally avoiding the formal approach.

All of them were informed about the founding of the club by the word of mouth, that is, by a volunteer going door to door, as well as by letter when the date for the meeting was set. Those that came expressed that they expected a new feeling of togetherness to arise from this form of neighborhood organization, that they hoped people would start to care for each other and have more concern about their block as a whole. Getting to know each other seemed more important for the beginning than any kind of concrete action. (They wore name tags because many did not know others even by name!) In an informal atmosphere where there was no strict agenda and where people could relax while tasting cookies and sipping coffee, everybody soon opened up.

from an inner-city blue-collar
neighborhood.

Unless deliberate decisions are made by the [neighborhood] group to expand the techniques of the trade, those techniques (such as running a meeting, writing a leaflet, running a mimeo machine, being picket captain, etc.) will remain the property of a few "experts," who tend gradually, and frequently without realizing it, to exclude the rank-and-file members from a real role in the organization.

Martin Oppenheimer and
George Lakey,
A Manual for Direct Action
(Chicago; Quadrangle Books,
1964), p. 45

3 | **Leadership Resources:** Who Organizes?

A. VOLUNTARY ASSOCIATIONS AND NEIGHBORHOOD LIFE

For a neighborhood to become organized effectively, it needs to use the tools of bureaucracy without the form. If the neighborhood is the antidote to bureaucracy, what is the vehicle for preserving its character and yet staying flexible? To resist being controlled it needs to borrow some of the skills of its rival. What are these tools? Specialized knowledge about problems.

If the sewage plant is to be stopped from purchasing the property next door, if delinquency is rampant, strategies must be devised. Specialized expertise is the answer—either from within the neighborhood or from the community at large. Residents of other neighborhoods are sometimes members of the leadership cadre of the larger society. If the expertise is not available locally, then it must be borrowed or hired. There are specific ways in which this is done.

The most frequently used neighborhood strategy to get the advantages of formal organization and still be a unique base of informal ties is to set up "voluntary associations." Such a group as "Concerned Citizens Dealing with Delinquency" can act as a "halfway house" in its organizational form. It is small and flexible enough, representative enough (let us hope) to convey the concerns and goals of the neighborhood. Yet it has a continuity and often the "specialized leadership" and knowledge found in the bureaucratic structure. It is an ideal not readily attained.

Very often the local block club or neighborhood association is a reflection of the style and needs of its local area. No two are exactly alike. In fact, what often happens is that the local association undergoes a transformation according to the needs and "pulls" of its leaders and the social patterns of the neighborhood.

Before we can fully evaluate the significance of a level of participation in voluntary associations, we have to look at several things. First, we have to know the functions that the group performs for the individual and for the society. In addition, we have to find out about the existing structure of that organization—whether it is a very formal or a relatively informal one. Knowledge of the stated or intended purposes of the organization is another requisite. Does it have a single and constant goal or several goals? Is it more successful in pursuing one kind of goal than another?

Functions of Voluntary Associations

Let us examine those functions that voluntary associations can fill in the lives of individuals:

1. An integrative or socialization function, that is, an attempt to develop group goals, community or societal cohesion.
2. A prestige-conferring role which is an important part of determining individual career advancement, as well as indicating to people that they are on their way to becoming members of a group by participating in the organizations associated with that group or class.
3. A problem solving role aimed at dealing with specific issues which arise and which affect individuals and their daily lives.
4. "Expressive" activities, dealing with recreation, tension-release, and various forms of sociability.[1]

Typically, local voluntary associations can have a multiple character in that they can play all these roles. But the clear implication is that organizations are vital not only for the individual but also for a community in its need to adapt and survive.

Just because an organization is local in character does not mean it is flexible, responsive, or democratic. The "grass-roots" system can be just as rigid and bureaucratic as the most impersonal, large-scale corporation or service agency. One of the neighborhood ethnographic observers in our research project reports of her experience:

> A woman volunteered her house, just for one meeting, at which four persons showed up. A member of the Board said openly at that meeting: "People would be encouraged to come to Executive Board meetings if they were held, excuse me, not in private homes." Since the meetings were not even held in his home recently, there is obviously an embarrassment to come to other people's homes, without regard to the fact that they have known each other for a long time.
>
> Though these people have interacted on a regular basis for years, the relationship has always been very one-sided, never extending to friendship. Of course, this is not the matter of being better or worse but of behaving according to a different set of cultural norms: in this case it is the notion that house is to guard family privacy and that business meetings are not an occasion for socializing.[2]

Yet even these "formalistic excesses which local groups may manifest fly in the face of the natural capacity of such organizations to avoid "red tape."

> The Council, however, uses informal channels in order to acquire some information or to make contacts. At one meeting it was observed that all of the present officers live on the "west side." Someone should be recruited from the other side. A woman was mentioned who knows some people there personally—she will make contacts "on the east side" for the president and find people who would be interested in cooperating.[3]

Neighborhood associations embrace so diverse a range of groupings that it becomes rather unproductive to speculate about the "ultimate purposes" of the organization. The four functions of voluntary associations may occur simultaneously, or we may be able as observers to note that, over time, some of these functions seem to be more important than others.

The term "organization" is one that should be treated very broadly indeed. Moreover, we should be very careful not to require that an organization's purposes always be explicit and self conscious. A good example of this arose during research the authors were conducting relative to school-community relations. During an interview with an elementary school principal in a predominantly southern white neighborhood, the topic of active local groups was discussed.

After giving some thought to a question about "community organization" the principal responded, "Oh, no, these people aren't very political." In this instance "organization" meant specific formal goals and politically focused activities. When the question was rephrased to say, "Do people around here seem to get together to do things?" the school principal immediately responded, "Oh yes, there is the Southerners' club. This is a group of people who meet in backyards and who often discuss various things going on in the community."

The principal then recognized that his definition of a "political" group was a rather formalistic one because the Southerners club was indeed a "parapolitical" organization. It did not have to be politically organized to deal with specific problems or with specific political activities. But it certainly represented a potential source of discussing problems, clarifying opinions, interpersonal influence, and a whole array of expressions of community involvement which were basic to the nature of this particular southern white community.

Here's an example of that same "informal" style of organization in a black neighborhood:

> No, the only organizational activity seems to be *ad hoc*, to combat some nuisance.... There are things like the dope house, people banding together to do something about the dope house. In another case, that organization seems to have gone on for several years, on another nuisance type thing. There's an alcoholic father who every few years goes to a sanatarium, and while he's gone his kids throw big, wild parties. So they're organizing to the point where two or three of them are trying to buy them out—two or three people on that same block.
> The dope thing is really past, and this other thing comes up every so often. She said they had thought about organizing a block club. It would be for things like this, a more organized way of taking care of things like

this alcoholic thing. That's the kind of organization there
is—people get together for things like that. Or when the
sewers were flooding, they got together and went to City
Hall. It's not necessarily the same people doing this—it
seems to be all over. That seems to be the pattern, that
when something happens they get together. I can't tell
that there is any core group.[4]

Regardless of the formal or informal "style" of a
neighborhood association, one of the most basic and trouble-
some issues facing the neighborhood activist is: "When do I
go the organization route?" There are, of course, many "success" stories to shore up one's skepticism about neighborhood
organizations. Listen to this recitation of one such case in a
white suburban area:

The home-owners associations honor local business
with "good neighbor plaques," and the groups are
mutually supportive. Recently the Improvement Association was successful in bringing political and legal pressure to bear to stop the licensing of teen-aged nightclubs
in the area. They are largely responsible for the health
and the character of the business community as they do
have a powerful influence in licensing and building
permit decisions due to their members' general involvement in the local political arena.

Besides these standing organizations, other political
groups arise to meet specific needs. Two issues have recently sparked such organizations. The opposition to the
city administration crystallized into a petition recall attempt of the mayor headed by a city-wide committee to
remove the mayor centered locally at the Northeast
News offices and receiving the official support of the
homeowners' associations and the business association
and the unofficial support of the police community relations committee and the local City Hall.

Homeowners groups brought petitions door-to-
door and shops kept them on display while the paper
published a running total. The second issue was proposed school bussing for desegregation, opposition to
which spawned the new Mothers for Education Committee. The women involved in forming this group came
primarily from defunct Homeowners' Associations and a
church.

The group grew to encompass the entire northeast
and staged a large march and rally in mid-summer,

where veterans' groups, the homeowners', the business associations, and local politicians spoke out against busing. The group has been meeting in the local City Hall, dressed in red, white and blue, and is highly respected. They base their campaign on an appeal to American freedom of choice to go to the school of your choice and stress the educational and safety issues in busing.[5]

Voluntary Associations Come in Many Forms

There is potential risk in the form ultimately associated with any given voluntary association. Will the association become too rigid? Will it merely serve as a temporary diversion? The ways in which voluntary associations adapt to either neighborhood or membership characteristics will ultimately affect achievement of action goals.

Voluntary associations are inherently selective in their membership. They cannot coerce people to participate. Thus, they can end up being very unrepresentative and usually run by a small "oligarchy" of very dedicated and faithful members.[6] In fact, one of the worse consequences of setting up such an organization is its success! As it grows in membership, it gets more formal, less flexible, and the chances for real individual participation are reduced.

Basically, the voluntary neighborhood association will work very well if the small active group can speak for the interests of others not involved in it. That can only happen naturally if the neighborhood is very homogeneous—the local PTA does not include everyone, but there is virtually automatic expression of the interests of the whole neighborhood—a kind of silent majority—always present. More often, however, the neighborhood association itself sets the conditions for its smooth (or relatively smooth) functioning by adapting in one or more of several ways. This adaptation can be in terms of enforced homogeneity, structural change, or goal shifting.[7]

Enforced Homogeneity

This can be of two kinds: "selective recruitment" or "selective expulsion," and it involves the organization's sifting and sort-

ing of its membership. In this process, various status characteristics of members become salient in terms of defining
whether the group can function in a cohesive manner. If
individuals are very different in terms of age or social class,
the possibilities for internal conflict are increased. The organization reduces this by selectively seeking out particular
individuals with similar social status. In some sense, we might
refer to this as a kind of elitism, in that it keeps the membership fairly exclusive. In addition, "selective recruitment"
serves to limit the size of the organization, to attract members
who have similar characteristics, and to exclude those who do
not conform to the norms of the organization.

Here is a good instance from one of our neighborhood
research sites:

> Two [local] groups have a large active membership
> that is younger than that of the standing organizations.
> The younger adults are not joining the older groups but
> put their efforts during short crisis periods more in-
> tensely into special interest and problem-oriented
> groups. The new organizations tend to have the same
> organizational structure as the older groups, functioning
> with officers and a steering committee in a hierarchical
> fashion, but the steering committee, of necessity, is more
> responsive to members' desires due to the high level of
> mobilization and the result is a less oligarchic, more col-
> lective decision-making process. This is also due in part
> to the preponderance of women in their thirties and
> forties active in these new groups as opposed to the
> homeowners' associations, run by sixty-year old men.
> These women also more often come from a Catholic,
> Polish or Italian background while the older groups are
> controlled by the German Protestant population. The
> young Catholic women have had much experience run-
> ning collective actions in the church and have brought
> this to bear with energy to the present issues.[8]

These processes need not be formalized by rules or
explicit statements of exclusivity. However, over time an organization may be shown to have a membership with a
homogeneous composition even though we know that the organization is capable of drawing upon a diverse population.

Structural Adaptations

A second means by which organizations may respond to new needs is to alter its structure. This may take a variety of forms. One of these has to do with altering the way in which the leadership of the organization functions. For example, leaders may take on the special skills of knitting together a diverse membership. In this sense, the leadership may need to develop "social-emotional," "expressive," or "integrative" skills.[9] These enable leaders to develop cohesion in the groups even though individual members of the organization may in fact have many differences of opinion and outlook.

Often leadership itself becomes a basis for adaptation in terms of the types of personalities of the leaders and their "style of leadership." The question arises as to whether the leader should press for the accomplishment of specific tasks or whether he or she should stress the skills necessary for relating to the divergent members of the group. In the heterogeneous group the leader often must do both things effectively.

The structure of an organization may be related to its membership in terms of formalization. If the organization is extremely diverse in its membership, there may be a greater need to have special rules governing the behavior of members, election procedures, the division of labor within the organization, who shall take on special roles. etc. All of these aspects, which make the organization more formalistic, are required because the membership itself is so diverse that the usual informal means of communication and establishing of procedures are ineffective.

In addition, if an organization wants to relate to heterogeneous membership, provision must be made for special ways to handle conflicts. This might be subcommittees, negotiating groups, grievance committees, or any sort of mechanism which recognizes the possibility of internal conflict and the need for the organization to have built-in methods for dealing with this conflict.

Finally, an organization which is diverse in character may recognize that no set of formal administrative or structural arrangements will deal fully with the special problems of that structure and that the real need is to maintain a *flexibility* in structure in order to facilitate informal means of exercising power. In this sense, the organization may stress the need to have a lot of informal contact before meetings, a chance for people to relate to one another, to know how to modify what would otherwise be incompatible positions, and in various ways to insure that the anticipation of conflict may tend to reduce its disruptive influence on the organization.

"Goal Displacement"

There is a third process which has been elaborately discussed in various studies of larger- and smaller-scale bureaucracies. This is the process of "goal displacement." Simply stated, this means that any organization which starts out with a single goal, particularly one that is general in nature, is likely to find that over a period of time, the focus will shift from the original goal. Thus, the large-scale welfare bureaucracy, which seeks to serve the needs of the poor, may find that after some time, the basic need served is to create a new class of professional or high-prestige occupational roles.

The process of goal displacement means that the day-to-day operations of an organization, even a small voluntary association, are liable to produce a gradual shift in the emphasis of its activities from those focused on at first. In the heterogeneous organization, goal displacement results in a stress on what we might call 'instrumental activities,' i.e. the accomplishment of specific political and social goals. This is a shift in emphasis from its earlier goal of keeping the group united. This indicates that often an organization, in order to function, needs to provide a mixture of very specific activities along with those aspects of sociability and warm interaction which are necessary for any human group. In Chart 3 we have summarized the major ways that an organization adapts to its neighborhood environments.

Robert Michels—the renowned political theorist—once enunciated the "iron law of oligarchy"—stating that all organizations end up in the hands of a few dominant individu-

Chart 3
Modes of Voluntary Association Adaptation to Neighborhood Membership

I. Selective Recruitment-Expulsion	II. Structural Adaptation	III. Goal Displacement
a. Elitism—keep small and be exclusive	a. Give leadership different functions than in other situations; centralize, select leader on special criteria	a. Develop different goals for diverse interest groups in organization
b. Select leaders or members based on similarity with others in group	b. Formalize roles—rules, division of labor, etc.	b. Frequently shift goals or innovate with different programs
c. Members who are deviant are ostracized and excluded	c. Provide special formal mechanisms to handle conflict	c. Emphasize goals that are integrative for the group rather than instrumental
	d. Use informal power to deal with conflict	

als.[10] Yet the history of groups suggests equally an "iron law of democracy"—that challenge to the "older order" is as predictable as the fact that a small minority who once were "outsiders" become "insiders" given time and dedication to their cause. The dynamics of keeping a neighborhood organization alive and responsive to people's needs are important bases for evaluation where the action is or should be. And it is important to look beyond the immediate personalities of those currently "running the show." For behind their efforts are some group dynamics thay may recur again and again—new faces but the same plot.

B. NEIGHBORHOOD LEADERSHIP: WHO'S WHO IN THE LOCAL "ESTABLISHMENT" AND THE "UNDERGROUND"

Organizations tell part of the story of citizen action. But the individuals who become active can shape and alter the "system" of local power.[11] We have described the "structures" in which they can operate. Now let us focus on patterns of "visible" and formalized leadership roles of organization versus more informal patterns. One level consists of officers in various kinds of voluntary organizational settings, including local neighborhood groups (e.g., block clubs, PTAs, etc.). By asking whether people have "ever held an office or position of leadership in groups," we were able to follow up with a special interview given to current officers of local organizations.

A second level or strata of leadership is not very visible when one's perspective is from the top down. This more or less invisible leadership strata was discovered by asking: "Is there someone around this area who is an active person if you want to get something done?" For those people mentioned (designated as neighborhood activists), a special interview was conducted. We probed to discover the strategies and techniques used, and we found great variation from one neighborhood to another. Three local-leader roles stand out:

1. *The Neighborhood Activist:* This is a person who has a reputation for taking action but is not a member of an organization. Some neighborhoods have many of these individuals.

In some cases one activist knows another, and there is a structure. In other instances each activist has their own sphere of influences. Such individuals may often have no formal roles. Even when they do, their "leadership" legitimacy is a function of reputation, not structural position.

2. *Officers of Local Organizations:* This represents a type of formal leadership where the individual is elected or appointed. Such individuals may often have other informal leadership roles, but their basic legitimacy comes from the block club, PTA, or other organization in which they serve.

3. *Opinion Leaders:* These individuals may be "back-fence" helpers or specialists in some capacity. This type of person typically is approached frequently for advice or knowledge about a particular problem. Such a person may offer help, advice, or give information about where to get further help. As a norm setter and "referral agent" this type of leader is usually not part of a formal group.

Zeroing in on the Neighborhood Activist Role

The leadership system of a neighborhood can be just as varied as that in any other organization. In fact, our studies of the people who have a reputation for "getting things done" in neighborhoods show they are not necessarily the officers of block clubs, or representatives of parent-teacher groups or the local church.

It is helpful to think of two layers of neighborhood leadership—one at a formal level and one at an informal level. The first consists largely of people who have official positions in recognized local organizations, the second are "grass-roots" activists who may not be affiliated with any group at all. We find that the layers overlap and in some neighborhoods closely intertwine. In others they are quite separate. One may be very highly developed in a neighborhood—the other very inadequate and sparse. Whatever the pattern, each has a special role to play in mobilizing and carrying out the work of representing the needs and concerns of a neighborhood.

We want to give special attention to the informal level because that is always so easily overlooked in the assessment of who is a leader and what resources of leadership a neighborhood has. Often this layer of reputational leaders is invisible to the outside world. In many instances, these leaders do not even recognize their own role. There may be several of them living in the same neighborhood who don't know one another. Frequently they have a small following in the very immediate block or only one part of the neighborhood.

It is usually true that in order to discover and relate to such individuals a person must be close to the action of the neighborhood and become familiar with its day-to-day concerns. No outside bureaucratic agency can "create" such leaders. By trying to draw on such people to help with problems, such agencies—even those with no desire to "co-opt"—grass-roots leaders may destroy the credibility and natural role of the informal neighborhood activist.

The division of labor which often appears between "formal" and "informal" leaders follows a particular pattern: (1) in black neighborhoods, women tend more often to be the formal leaders, while men are more often the informal leaders; (2) in the white community, the reverse tends to be true—women are more likely to be informal leaders, while men tend to assume the formal leadership roles.[12]

In many instances in the neighborhoods we studied, the same individual is *both* a neighborhood activist and an officer in an organization. This kind of dual role was more rare in black neighborhoods than in white neighborhoods. Overall, this kind of individual serves as an important link between community organizations, the formal structure of neighborhoods and the informal leadership configuration.

One basic question we asked informal activists was the following: "How about your own role in community activities? Which do you do most?" People could indicate a range from acting to "calm people down, make everyone relax," to "set up . . . the things the group is trying to do" with variations in-between. From research conducted by Freed Bales and others, two major "styles" of leadership have been identified: a "task"-oriented role (setting goals and providing answers to a group) and "expressive" (giving emotional support and encouragement). Successful group dynamics have been found to generally require both types of leadership to solve problems—although not necessarily in the same person. Our research suggests that the same is true for neighborhood activists.

Why People Become Activists

In our research exploring how the neighborhood activist (the informal local leader) functions, we asked the over 400 individuals their reasons for getting involved.[13] Specifically, the kinds of satisfactions they felt differed and so did the rewards. But certain themes emerged. Personal helping and the sense of reward from completing a job and showing their skills in influencing others were foremost motivations. Often such activities were a substitute for a dead-end or nonchallenging job. Frequently neighborhood activists said they wanted to take their mind off some problem in their life which was bothering them and had no immediate solution.

Less frequently mentioned by neighborhood activists is the satisfaction of social bridge building and sociability rewards. Sometimes these reasons are couched in social-mobility and status-striving terms—"being known in the community"—but as often people said they just enjoyed "meeting new people."

We can sum up these motivations under the general label of personal effectiveness. By serving as part of a natural helping network, neighborhood activists were telling us how a community survives and prospers. Yet the role of the informal neighborhood activist is first and foremost a personal triumph in self-reward. It need not be necessary to consider each activist as a self-conscious member of the neighborhood leadership cadre. The very anonymity and informality in style of many activists is the key to their success and enjoyment of their role.

By being part of a very visible and manageable community, they derive a sense of genuine participation and belonging. For many neighborhood activists being a "big fish in a small pond" means just being known on their immediate block. The lines of leadership are short and do not necessarily intertwine. Just as the perspective of relatedness becomes apparent when we stand at a distance from an intricate painting, so does the pattern of neighborhood leadership become evident when one steps back from the social circle of each reputational activist. The many short paths of activists often form a layer covering all or most parts of many neighborhoods.

One important note: only 5 percent of all residents named the same neighborhood activists—the other 95 percent of elementary-school-district residents tend to name different activists distributed throughout the neighborhood. In other words, in a neighborhood of one thousand households, the same activist might be known at most to perhaps forty or fifty families living in that neighborhood. This is indeed a modest political constituency! Yet, it is also a very meaningful unit upon which to build neighborhood action.

Links between Layers—A Good Idea or Not?

We find that one major aspect of the structure of leadership in a neighborhood is the degree to which informal activists know each other and, in turn, whether they are known by persons who are formal leaders of local groups. In some situations formal leaders not only know who informal leaders are, but they themselves turn out to be people in both roles. They are known widely as leaders, yet this is not simply because they hold an office in some local group.

Such a tight neighborhood "infrastructure" is relatively rare. More often, informal leaders and formal leaders are partly separate layers of the structure of a neighborhood. The character of the neighborhood in terms of ethnic, social class, and residential stability all affect how divergent or how solidary is the structure of leadership.

There are many examples where outside agencies—by not knowing about reputational activists—found a program or policy subverted because they did not understand the role or attempt to work with such key people. In still other cases they sought to draw on such persons only to find that their "power" was really a subtle blend of advice giving and simply being around in time of need. They could not introduce a new idea but they could certainly be a barrier to a school principal's pet project or a police community-relations program. In fact, one of the major functions performed by informal leaders is protecting the neighborhood from outside interference and manipulation.

Because each style of leadership is unique and has a special place in the life of a neighborhood as a community, "loose" ties between different kinds of leaders are not themselves negative aspects of a neighborhood. Indeed, there is much evidence to show from the motivations of people who are reputational activists that success in invading their "turf" or putting them into a wider arena of influence or recognition results in destruction of the very fabric of neighborhood organizations which they represent. This fine web of "indigenous leadership" may be destroyed if it is called upon too often and treated as a "professional" or "representative" group. Such individuals seldom really are typical of their neighborhood. Often they are older or longer tenure residents.

The neighborhood organizer's problem frequently is not one of seeking to tap the leadership or to develop a capacity for influence and action in the organizations and the individuals found in the local neighborhood but instead to seek to more effectively link-up and correlate the diversity of structures and processes of leadership that may already exist. It is not, therefore, fundamentally a question of *developing* leadership as much as it is one of *coordinating* that leadership.

Knowing that a neighborhood is rich in informal leadership resources may be far from a blessing for the person who seeks social change or neighborhood mobilization. The usual assumption of "mobilizing" leaders can turn out to be a distracting and costly strategy. Make no mistake: an effective neighborhood activist can be an invaluable ally. But the major principle to bear in mind is to avoid taking such individuals out of the context of their leadership role. By co-opting or converting them their role may be totally subverted. To be effective in neighborhood action, one often must relate simultaneously to divergent and unrelated layers of neighborhood leadership. This need not entail uniting them, although that may be feasible and even very desirable at some later point. What becomes increasingly clear about the dynamics of neighborhood action is that different leaders often function in relation to different problems and constituencies.

Before embarking on the primary focus of "uniting the neighborhood for action," one must carefully assess the risk that bringing together divergent leadership elements may exaggerate just how little common basis for action exists in a neighborhood. Later, we shall discuss more fully how neighborhoods with a high degree of variability in their composition cannot be approached in the same way as those neighborhoods having a natural commonality of interest.

In Sum: Neighborhoods Have Varieties of Leadership

We began this chapter with a discussion of leadership roles. We have relied heavily on our analysis of the Detroit area data to point out what seemed to be some of the structural differences in the pattern of leadership as it occurs at the "middle level" of political organization—that is, the informal neighborhood activist and the officer of a voluntary association. In identifying the richness and variety of such leadership resources, we have also pointed out that this may imply sharply different strategies of organization in the black ghetto as compared with either the low-income white neighborhood or the middle-class white community.

By carefully defining the character of the problem at hand, it may become necessary to differentiate *which kind of leadership structure* is to be activated in solving a given problem. If the issue is, for example, one concerned with cooperation between organizations located in one neighborhood versus another, it is clear thay many of the formal structures which exist in neighborhoods are not likely to have easy access to other organizations, and particular efforts to create a coalition must be introduced. At the same time, there is evidence that, on the informal level of leadership, there may well be a great deal of contact between individuals active both in organizations and on the outside. In fact, the same individual may be able to take the goal of an organization which they may agree with and carry it to individuals who are not active in that particular group. Furthermore, such individuals may in fact have contacts beyond their immediate local neighborhood.

Organizer's Exercises
Chapter 3

ORGANIZATIONAL HISTORY OF THE NEIGHBORHOOD

a. What has been happening in this area that people are talking about, etc.? Are there some controversies where groups in the neighborhood have been active?

b. Has there been anything that has divided the area?

c. Have groups tended to be focused, specialized, and "task" oriented in character or "social-emotional," diffuse, or escapist? (Get as full a list of voluntary associations and formal organizations as possible. Informal groups are also of interest.)

d. Has any collective action been successful or unsuccessful?

e. How much do people know about other neighborhoods? (How many links to other groups and institutions outside of the local neighborhood do you find? This includes work, leisure, political, religion, or other spheres not locally focused.)

f. Are there organizational ties to specific other neighborhoods?

0	1	2	3	4	5	6	7	8	9
No ties								Many ties	

g. Names of organizations active in the area:
   1.
   2.
   3.
   4.
   5.
   6.

h. Are there identifiable leaders in the neighborhood?

i. Are they representative?

j. What are the characteristics of "good leaders"? (Character and social attributes, e.g., charisma, education, ties with the outside community.)

k. Is there any issue or problem where you organized a group effort or influenced others in some common action?

YES_____ NO_____

(IF YES) Exactly what was the problem?

Exactly what did you do?

l. What about you? What is most satisfying about being active in the community?

1. Allows you time to meet people
2. Allows you to speak and act on important issues
3. Gives you more information about the community
4. Gives you a chance to test your organizing skills
5. Gives you a feeling of being able to influence others
6. Gives you an added sense of personal worth
7. Makes you well known in the community (neighborhood)
8. Other:

m. How about your own role in community activities. Which of the following do you do most? Which comes next? (Place a "1" by the first choice and a "2" by the second choice)

_____1. Calm people down, make everyone relax, work to reduce tension
_____2. Set up and outline the things the group is trying to do
_____3. Back up good ideas, show how different ideas could fit together
_____4. Suggest ways in which the groups could best handle the problem at hand
_____5. Act only to clarify and encourage participation by others
_____6. Other:

Neighborhoods [can be seen] as underdeveloped nations. They now suffer from aspects of imperialism similar to those of the third-world countries: outside intervention in local affairs.

Morris and Hess,
Neighborhood Power, p. 14

Though neighboring communities overlook one another and crowing of cocks and barking of dogs can be heard, yet the people there may grow old and die without ever visiting one another.

Lao-tzu, *Tao te ching*

4 | **Reaching Out for Your Neighborhood:** Foreign Policy

We now return to the neighborhood organization "mission." Interestingly enough, not a great deal of guidance material is readily available on how, when, and why to organize neighborhoods.[1] The literature and discussion focuses on minority and low-income neighborhoods.[2] Even there the "job specifications" are loosely drawn. There are many good "role models" ranging from direct action "conflict strategies" to such concepts as the "enabler," and the goals to be carried out are described in terms such as "adaptation" and "culture building."[3]

Many of these expectations and requirements grow out of the formal training in schools of social work.[4] Professionalization of the organizer is one of the major trends of our contemporary society's mania over how to solve social problems. What about a less formal approach? And how about looking at what neighborhood activists—as defined by their neighbors—actually do, *not* what a theoretical treatise suggests that they ought to do?

Except in very small rural communities most neighborhood activists find themselves part of a complex and highly varied set of human institutions. Very often these institutions seem to fit into a kind of pecking order—a hierarchy of strata—often dominating the life of the individual citizen. These vertical "layers" of the community can be separated according to the differences between a series of key leaders and heads of powerful organizations—a "power elite"—comprised of professionals, administrators in bureaucratic organizations, and the welter of voluntary associations that cross cut the neighborhoods of any community. Sometimes these blend together and merge as one: "the establishment."

73

In other instances, these segments are very loosely related or totally separate centers of power and privilege.

A basic mission of any neighborhood activist is to (1) identify each segment and (2) decide how most effectively to relate to or protect against these "outside" forces which directly or indirectly determine the fate and fortune of neighborhood action. Perhaps the analogy of Morris and Hess is not so very off the mark: let us consider—if neighborhoods are "nations"—what the "foreign-policy" role of the activist/organizer should be: isolationism, negotiation, coexistence, detente, or conflict.

In this chapter we will approach these issues in a generic way and then in chapter 6 return to the "foreign policy" of local activists functioning in specific kinds of neighborhoods.

A. RELATING TO THE "POWER ELITE"

Morris and Hess have described the process of "intercommunalism,"[5] that is, where neighborhoods begin by looking inward and trying to develop their human resources. A second stage then occurs which is one of outward orientation. This kind of development is partially a result of economic factors, but it also stems from a growing awareness that the neighborhood lacks political power and faces the inevitable frustration of dealing with petty bureaucrats and overspecialized experts. The neighborhood residents begin to see themselves as one tiny cog in a very complex economic, political, and social system.

This is the beginning, then, of outreach and linkage efforts. Who has the power in the larger community? Any discussion with activists involves some need to assess the top layers of community influence. There have been a number of studies concerning the identification of those people who really control the reins of power. In addition, there is a vast literature describing the different forms that the power process takes. The question is that posed by Martin Oppenheimer in his manual for direct action, namely, "which people, families and business concerns, which politicians, ministers, and educators have the authority to make decisions which influence behavior of other individuals or groups?"

Generally speaking, the real decision power resides in those with the highest status positions. This is also the case when we are dealing with minority communities that may have miniature elites to match those of the dominant community. This was one of the points made by Floyd Hunter in *Community Power Structure* when he studied black and white systems of elite influence in Atlanta, Georgia, in the 1950s.[6]

The fact that there will be a concentration of influence is a major point. In the classic study by C. Wright Mills of the *Power Elite*,[7] he also described a second very fundamental process, that is, the social cohesion of those "at the top." They have gone to certain schools and universities, they live in a particular neighborhood themselves, they belong to the same social clubs, attend certain churches, and above all, they are concentrated in particular occupations and professions, particularly law, banking, and large business management.

Obviously, the power group varies somewhat from community to community. The important point is that the neighborhood activist must be able to reach this group in order to tap its power. This may not occur at the initial stage of dealing with a problem or issue, but almost inevitably it will come up at some point in the process.

As Si Kahn describes it, a good organizer is always able to size up the opposition, and to this extent, he suggests that it is a good idea never to underestimate people that are opposed to you. Especially with organizers working in lower power communities and neighborhoods, he argues, there is a certain "conning" of the power structure by which the organizer attempts to gain its confidence.[8] This is not necessarily overt or conscious deception. While the organizer may believe that what he is trying to accomplish is in the long run best for the total community, he or she also has to recognize that it is often contrary to what the power structure sees as its own best interests.

A good organizer always assumes the other side is using all the tactics that the organizer is using and using them at least as well. Further, while the power elite has slightly different shape and composition from one community to another, it is important to recognize that it is indeed divided, that it seldom has a unified front, and that this difference and conflict can be used by the neighborhood activist.

But it is clear that regardless of the threat posed by interacting with the power elite, consciously avoiding it is generally a critical mistake. Some sort of contact—whether initiated by the power elite or by the local activist—should be followed up, and the maintenance of some continuous contact provided, even though there are dangers and cautions involved.

Researchers who have studied organizations and small groups have found that the person who is most likely to be at the margins of the group is also the one most likely to have contacts with other organizations and thus become a "bridge." At the same time such individuals themselves are generally in some way status inconsistent, that is, they have characteristics which sometimes closely resemble the group that they are representing, and at other times they are closer to characteristics of the outside group. It is exactly this kind of marginality which gives this sort of person the special skills as a foreign emissary. The danger is that the individual with those kinds of conflicting expectations may come under a great deal of psychological stress and strain.

It is not hard to imagine a person who represents her/his neighborhood organization in a battle to encourage zoning enforcement agreeing with contacts in the wider community that group homes for the handicapped are good and necessary.

At the same time, the discussion of the role of the "marginal-linking" individual is one which emphasizes the capacity to innovate and to serve as a stimulator of new ideas. Traditional social psychology of group leadership has stressed the fact that leaders are allowed to deviate from the group norms more than rank-and-file members are. One of these deviations has to do with contact with the "enemy." It is precisely in this foreign-policy role in interacting with the power elite that the neighborhood leader comes to risk a loss of legitimacy.

Si Kahn puts the matter in a slightly different way. He sees that the power structure is very effective at defining its own interests and will quickly see any threat that is posed to it by a local organizer and move to head that effort off. In turn, the organizer is the one who will be most in danger of being "conned" by the power structure.[9]

There is more to be said beyond subtle or cunning political maneuvering regarding the advantages and dangers of mixing with the power elite. On the negative side, there is the fact that many organizers or activists in particular groups become, after a time, under the control of the power structure's interpretation of the problem. They begin to identify with that elite and lose their attachment to the local neighborhood.

Thus, the great danger in prolonged contact with the power elite is the subtle or blatant co-optation. Edmund Burke defines co-optation as the "process of absorbing new elements into the leadership or policy determining structure as means of averting threats to its stability and existence."[10] But how does one confront the issue of co-optation and avoid it when necessary?

From another perspective, many of those who have worked in community action efforts of various kinds perceive that the basic danger of contact with the power elite has to do with the role of the organizer as he faces his own local constituents. The actual danger of being co-opted by the power structure is not as great as the *perceived danger* that the organizer has been co-opted. Thus, the image of the organizer which is held by her/his neighbors becomes a critical basis of leadership legitimacy. Once that is lost, once distrust emerges, then it is clear that the role of the neighborhood activist has been seriously undermined.

Some of the research we have carried out has underscored the fact that such a danger is greatest when community alienation is very high. Part of this depends on the leader's source of authority and expertise; does it arise from the local community or has he/she been hand-picked by the power elite and put in a position of authority in the community? Many of the federal programs, Model Cities efforts, and a wide range of other organizations that are called "grass roots" are really in fact creations of dominant agencies and elites. When the neighborhood representatives are appointed by the power elite, the bases of their leadership roles are suspect. The professional administrator of a program such as a social service agency, a staff member of the human-rights organization, or a scout leader have leadership positions in the neighborhood. But the bases of their leadership roles derive not from their activities within the neighborhood but from their position as created by these outside organizations.

Neighborhood Internal Structure and the Linking Role

Our research findings show such a danger is especially great in a minority community. One reason for this is that the very ghettoization of minorities is accompanied by a clustering of people of diverse social-status levels in the same neighborhood. Black neighborhoods more often than white are, therefore, found to be status diverse: Black people with high and low education, income, and other characteristics are living cheek by jowl.[11]

One consequence of neighborhood status diversity is that status levels become blurred, lifestyle cannot be asserted in a clear and distinctive pattern, and the very basis of high and low status is lost in the complexity of population groupings. If the individual's unclear status position is coupled with taking on an intermediary role between local interest groups and outside power centers, the resulting strain on that person is so great as to reduce willingness to step into such a leadership-bridging position. In the neighborhood where many social characteristics are clear and the leadership role does not involve conflicting expectations, it is easier to find a cadre of people willing and able to assume leadership roles.

Such a leadership situation is analogous to a person from a Third World country who is educated at Oxford, Cambridge, Harvard, or Berkeley, and once out of his community finds that he no longer has a role there; in fact, he no longer sees himself in relation to that home-of-origin community. This displacement of leadership to the larger community and the resulting loss to the neighborhood is a major resource problem particularly for the "foreign policy" of any very heterogeneous neighborhood.

The more heterogeneous the neighborhood and community in values, lifestyles, and goals, the more likely it is that leaders will emerge on the basis of a special issue or representing a special segment of the neighborhood. The broad-scale, universal sort of leadership role is usually reserved for those who have led the group to a significant victory or who have a well-established basis of accomplishment. Thus the neighborhood activist should realize that some initial small-scale victory must be obtained. These can be relatively minor issues—the location of a stop sign, for example—or they may be of a more visible significant level—the challenge of a school policy, the replacement of an administrator, or the addition of a new program in a local school. The major point is that delivery of the goods becomes a basis for attaining legitimacy.

Some neighborhoods can absorb their internal diversity because there are enough leadership and other resources to go around. They can afford the luxury of legitimizing a wide variety of goals and values. Often, in the middle-class setting, the interests of different members of the neighborhood are much more articulately developed than in a lower-income area. As a result, effective performance and trust in such a setting is likely to be based not on the personal appeal of the leader but instead upon the specific accomplishments and resources that the individual brings to bear. Often, in an early phase of community and neighborhood development, the need for magnetic leadership to stimulate people out of their apathy and motivate them to take action requires the magnetic personality.

Frequently, however, this wears thin, and even though there may be a gradual shift in the kinds of activities the leader is involved in, the basic role pattern is maintained. If the neighborhood activist starts out providing stimulating rhetoric and an effective attack on the power elites' control over the neighborhood or the specific evils of such manipulation, there may be no development of the issue toward changing the power situation. Instead, the leader gets co-opted in a subtle way by the power elite. Because he or she is able to talk strongly to the elite, there is a danger of being taken in as the token radical, used to sooth the consciences of the elite groups, and, often in a fairly sophisticated manner, being manipulated by that elite group to its own interests.

An organizer's role or relationship involving the power-holders in a community must be highly differentiated. There may have to be several points of contact with the power elite. Very often a neighborhood's problems are caused directly or indirectly not by collusion between those who have charge of governmental or other agencies but by ignorance of the impact that their decisions have on the neighborhood. There are, of course, exceptions; but it is often very difficult to distinguish between disorganization and conspiracy. Many banks, business and civic groups, and even schools are able to manipulate a neighborhood in ways that are detrimental to its best interest, not because of a conscious policy but because of the lack of awareness of how their policies impinge on a given neighborhoods. It becomes one of the most important jobs of the neighborhood activist not to provide the rhetoric activism but to serve as a significant definer of the neighborhood's problems and to recognize that the major concern is the functional outcome of various institutions and their decisions—whether it is the schools, the police, the highway commission, the zoning boards, or other major groups.

It is not a matter of attacking the power elite for its motivations, and extolling the virtues of the neighborhood, but of pointing out the points of contact and exploitation occurring partly because the power elite itself is insulated from the organizations over which it holds dominance. It was important for Mill's conceptualization of the power elite that he saw that the social similarity of those who manage corporations, social agencies, and various other large-scale bureaucracies was based in part on the growing uniformity of all bureaucratic systems. A basic element of such growth is the tremendous problem of the upward flow of communication and information.

Thus, even the enlightened administrator and corporate executive may simply not know what is going on at the grass roots. Therefore, the neighborhood activist often is in the position not of "conning" the power elite but of educating the power elite as to what their organizations are doing to a neighborhood.

As in foreign policy in general, infiltration and counterespionage are often exciting pastimes which indeed may yield results. But seldom are these results readily controllable. And as happens with those who are more experienced in the game of international espionage recognize, it is almost impossible to tell who is on which side. People change sides in a kind of musical chairs, which is bewildering and impossible for the citizen to accept let alone understand.

Thus, we must put aside the concern with undercover and counterinsurgency strategies in relating the neighborhood to the power elite and, instead, consider a series of more specific and overt problems regarding the flow of information. First, it is crucial to define situations in a language which can be shared by those experiencing a problem as well as those with the resources to do something about it. Second, the maintenance of contacts is necessary to provide continuity with and accountability for the policies of large, impinging organizations. Third, and perhaps most important, the neighborhood activist must be willing to step aside in favor of others who have more effective skills in dealing with the powerful. Finally, a leader cannot afford to be so engrossed in external contact that grass-root contacts in the community become imperiled. To be effective in the wider arena, a neighborhood leader must be in close touch with the neighborhood itself.

B. RELATING TO THE BUREAUCRATIC "ESTABLISHMENT"

In chapter 3 we discussed some of the dilemmas that the organizer or activist faces when trying to use voluntary associations as a mechanism of problem solving. In that discussion, we talked about some inherent tendencies of organizations to become more formal as they grow in size as well as the fact that voluntary associations rely very heavily on a sort of automatic homogeneity of their membership or constituents. In light of these organizational dynamics, it becomes very difficult to describe the ideal strategy for relating to organizations. Clearly, it is a very good situation to have a neighborhood leader who is also involved with one or more community-wide associations.

Most often, effective bridging relationships which link the neighborhood to a wider organizational network are achieved not between a local group within the neighborhood and affiliated counterparts elsewhere in the community, but rather through individuals. Such persons serve as "common messengers" facing in two directions at once, providing information to the neighborhood about what is occurring in other organizations and, at the same time, bringing the neighborhood's point of view to bear in meetings of groups found outside the neighborhood.

In order to use the balance theory or linkage theory effectively, a community or neighborhood activist must make two different diagnoses. First of all, with regard to any formal agency or bureaucracy, there must be a decision in terms of whether to become more closely tied to—or more distant from—that organization. In the first instance, it is a matter of establishing the kinds of ties that will permit the neighborhood to draw upon the special advantages of the formal specialized agency—its expertise, its efficiency, its capacity to get a message out very rapidly to a wide audience, as well as its ability to organize a great deal of knowledge and bring it to bear on a specific problem. On the other hand, whenever the neighborhood is seeking to define its interests or goals, there may be too close a relationship between an organization and a neighborhood. For example, if a school principal is in a position to control the PTA presidency, the result is a kind of control that may work against the best interest of the neighborhood.

The dangers of being too close or too far from the formal resources present very personalized sorts of problems. The important thing to remember is that they have to be recognized and dealt with and not left to trial and error. Using the Litwak-Meyer linkage notion of "balance,"[12] there are a number of particular techniques that can be used by the neighborhood activist in order to effectively relate to outside formal organizations and bureaucracies while minimizing the danger. The first is called the "advocate bureaucracy."[13] This is simply a strategy in which a miniature replica of the outside agency is built right within the neighborhood. Sometimes this occurs when an outside agency sets up a branch in the neighborhood. If the personnel in that branch are people who live in the neighborhood, the chances are that they will be more sensitive to its interests.

A second tactic is referred to by Litwak and Shiroi as a "delegated bureaucracy."[14] This involves the setting up of a part of the bureaucracy which has as its job responding to the interests of citizen's groups in the neighborhood. There is a rather elaborate experience with such entities in the Model Cities neighborhood program and more recently in the so-called Act-54 advisory board set up to deal with mental health. The advantage of these kinds of organizations is that they provide a clearly mandated channel between the outside associations and the local neighborhood.

The disadvantage of these kinds of strategies is that the definition of neighborhood is usually a very artificial one. Model Cities programs were based on artificially defined administrative units which were created by collecting all of the social problem data and carving out an area which maximized the argument for assistance. In other instances, an advisory council set up by such legislation as Act-54 provides for representation but usually on a community-wide basis. In this sense, community often means ethnic group. This, in turn, creates a basis for representation not in terms of geography but rather in terms of identities which may cut across geographical units.

The ombudsperson role and the negotiating role which various subunits of large-scale bureaucracies fulfill or the setting up of branch units of larger organizations are indeed important arenas in which the activist needs to be involved.

Neighborhood leaders can be creative in helping to institute such linkages. If the mechanisms are already there, the neighborhood leader can certainly participate at least to the extent of making known the neighborhood needs.

Links to City Hall: A Case in Point

Let's give an example of the linking strategy process. In an effort to redevelop a neighborhood in the city of Ann Arbor, Michigan, there was the need to call upon federal funds. According to legislative requirements, the city was the agent for the disbursement of funds to citizens or neighborhood groups. In this case, the issue was urban renewal. The funds were to be used to install storm, sewer, and indoor plumbing facilities or connections as well as improving the level of access to the neighborhood by paving undeveloped streets.

In the course of getting help for this neighborhood, it became clear that federal legislation placed very clear guidelines on what the city had to do. For one thing, it had a deadline for developing the basic information as to what were the needs of the neighborhood. This became the basis for qualifying to receive the necessary funds. Notoriously cumbersome and complex, this and other requirements under urban renewal and, later, Model Cities and other programs became barriers to swift and effective action. Delay and inaction provide no encouragement to current residents and their fears about the future.

But there was an important question which arose early in the discussion of urban renewal. Many residents were very fearful that urban renewal would mean a drastic change in their way of life and would end up costing them more money, reducing their property value, and resulting in an area which instead of having a kind of distinct rural character would in fact become part of a slum environment. The perceptual dimensions were extremely critical. A coordinator was introduced into the situation. This person really acted in the role of advisor to the citizens of the area. Hired by the city, it was his duty to provide the residents with access to information.

The initial problem was that residents felt left out of the decision making process. They did not really know what urban renewal might mean. Thus, initially, the coordinator was to convey information from city hall to the local neighborhood to correct myths and to squelch rumors that heightened fears and caused some to feel they must leave the neighborhood—despite major investments in their homes and attachments to that environment.

In turn, the city felt that it could no longer define, in terms of its mandate, what the character of changes in the neighborhood would be after the urban renewal improvements were put in place. It was clear that some kind of input from residents themselves, defining what their future should be, had to be obtained. As the controversy proceeded, one of the activities supported by the city coordinator was a survey of neighborhood residents. Here, city hall acted as the resource, channeling funds and expertise to the neighborhood, in terms of supporting the idea of a survey. In turn, city residents were also given the option to hire a consultant firm which would work along with the city and the local residents to determine the best set of physical plans to be developed for the neighborhood.

All of this proceeded on a basis of obtaining survey information from individuals. The resulting data was analyzed not simply in terms of federal definitions of substandard housing and health hazards but also in terms of the positive values which residents saw in their neighborhood. The residents' attitudes toward their neighborhood, the needs they regarded as crucial, and the suggestions they had for its improvement were introduced at the critical point of the decision, not merely to bring up to city code the sewer and water facilities of the neighborhood but to improve in some meaningful way the quality of the residential environment of the neighborhood.

This desire to maintain the character of the neighborhood by virtue of consulting with and drawing upon the views of residents permitted the city to reach its goal, which was to have safe and sanitary housing. At the same time neighborhood residents were able to ensure that their property values remained high and that in fact the kind of neighborhood they wanted was not going to be altered by the urban renewal grants.

In this case, the outcome was successful and positive, in contrast to many other such experiences. The survey enabled residents, through their consultants, to communicate with the experts of city hall about what kind of neighborhood they wanted. The language and aesthetic barriers had been crossed. Different forms of dialogue that are always involved when primary groups, with their distinct values, interact with formal organizations were synchronized by important intermediaries—the linking individuals—who were hired by the city to help residents. The outcome was that urban-renewal improvements were made and the neighborhood was significantly upgraded in terms of its necessary city services. Moreover, the creation of a plan which maximized the qualities inherent in the neighborhood resulted in a rather remarkable increase in the economic values of the neighborhood. Rather than being preceived as a rural peripheral slum, it is now renamed and redefined by many residents of the city as a whole—as well as its own residents—as a desirable environment, one of the unique elements of a diversified community.

Distinct from strategies directly linking outside bureaucratic resources is the organizer operating purely as an intermediary relating the outside organization only indirectly to the neighborhood. This might be a complaint letter, through asking for information and, on occasion, the bringing of a legal suit, or other kinds of activities to influence the outside organization.

There are many other linking kinds of strategies, some involving direct action and mass protest efforts. A less obvious strategy would be to contact a member of the neighborhood who holds a key position in a corporation or agency and relating to that person by using their influence once they have been informed of the problem at hand. In addition, there is the use of special people in the neighborhood who do not have particularly powerful roles in an organization, but who are essential to its maintenance. This might include people in the school system such as lunch-room attendants, street crossing guards, and people in other community positions such as the police department, the water works, the local media, etc. These are not really direct links, but neighborhood activists, by knowing of such individuals and relating to them, may be in a position to understand and to mobilize neighborhood concerns either to protect against the intrusion of that outside organization or to work toward altering the policies of that agency.

Another kind of strategy involves using very specialized kinds of people who are involved in some organizational auxillary, such as a church group or a PTA organization. Such people can be valuable in trying to communicate special needs of the neighborhood indirectly to outside organizations or bureaucracies.

An Overview of Neighborhood "Foreign Policy"

In this chapter we have reviewed some of the principles by which the neighborhood activist can decide on how to relate to specialized elite groups as well as to other neighborhood organizations and outside agencies. All of this is predicated on the notion that the neighborhood is in some sense unable to survive without some degree of interdependence with the larger community.[15]

First there is the question of how much of a "formal-strategy" activism is required and how much strictly on the basis of grass-roots expertise. There is no doubt that the degree of success for any activist effort depends on raising the question early in the process of participation. But a close second consideration is: "What are the costs and benefits of linkage with the outside world?" This is not a matter which involves only leadership roles or issues. It involves an understanding of the basic structure of neighborhood and that of the larger community and how the two are best interfaced to reach neighborhood goals.

Charles Grosser puts the issue as follows:

> The *sine quo non* of grass-roots organization is independence. But the survival and growth of any newly formed organization, especially one lacking the resources of power, money and knowledge, requires dependence on some individual organization that can supply the needed assets.[16]

This is not an easy nor readily available calculus. Instead, it requires some testing and comparison. Models of neighborhood types as well as the forms of information and principles of the way organizations work provide some of the working tools. But the job of the activist is to put them together in some meaningful whole. Most of all, the fact is that the activist has a major responsibility for providing the tie— either in a protective sense or in a problem-solving sense—for relating to the outside world. In the best sense of the word, the neighborhood activist very often is the emissary or the ambassador, and without understanding outside relationships, it will be impossible for the neighborhood activist to develop an effective and meaningful internal action program.

If, in fact, many groups find they must isolate themselves from some people who live in the local neighborhood, then what is the implication for their seeking to join with other groups beyond the local neighborhood? This presents the neighborhood activist with a dual problem: devising mechanisms for the coexistence of diverse in-neighborhood organizations or factions and at the same time being in a position to manifest unity to the outside.

The implication is clear: to the extent that local associations in the neighborhood do not represent their own area, the possibility of forming a pyramid of local groups and thereby creating a tight neighborhood cohesion is extremely limited. Even if it is granted that neighborhood organization is a crucial matrix within which to build community cohesion, the "critical mass" represented by a unit even as small as the elementary school district may be too diverse to be "represented" by a single voluntary association.

We have already discussed in chapter 3 that the building blocks of community which use neighborhood do not correspond with the patterns which we find characteristic of voluntary associations, especially as they are found in heterogeneous areas. As a result, if we wish to make a case for the role of building community from the neighborhood level up, one must take into account the extent of diversity in social structures found in a given neighborhood. It is to this task that we now turn.

**Organizer's Exercises
Chapter 4**

RELATING TO THE "POWER ELITE" AND THE "BUREAUCRATIC ESTABLISHMENT"[8]

a. *Form your own bureaucracy*
   A permanent group is formed to demand information or action from an agency or actually to take over the work of a service organization. Example: Kloman's Resource Center on Day Care.

b. *Ombudsman organization is used*
   Your community or State has an agency or unit that has a specific legal task to deal with grievances, consumer complaints, or violation of rights. Example: civil rights commission.

c. *Form an ad-hoc group*
   A group is formed dealing with a specific issue or a problem, and when it is dealt with, the group dissolves.

d. *Mass Actions*
   Marches, boycotts, or use of mass media to dramatize a problem.

e. *Using a local contact person*
   Someone who lives in the neighborhood who is working for an agency or organization you want to influence.

f. *Contacting former residents or peers who don't live in the neighborhood*
    You know a person who works in an organization and he shares
    your views or has a commitment to your goals.

g. *Using so-called para-professionals*
    Getting an organization to hire or use the services of local
    neighborhood people who are picked because they have "grass-
    roots" expertise, not bureaucratic credentials.

h. *Contacting Board Members*
    Going to individuals at top levels of an organization—especially
    if they are nearby residents—who set policy that the "bureau-
    crats" enforce.

i. *One-to-one "eyeball" contact*
    Going as a single individual to complain about a policy or rule of
    an organization.

MAKING THE MOST OF THE ORGANIZATIONAL
ESTABLISHMENT

1. In your position as an influential member of the community,
    people may come to you for advice. How about groups? Do
    organizations also come to you for advice on issues or actions?

    YES_____   NO_____

    (IF YES) Their coming to you implies that they value your
    judgment. Why do they feel that way?

    a. Your knowledge of their particular organization
    b. Your knowledge of organizations in general
    c. Your knowledge of the community
    d. Your knowledge, and thorough experience as to how things
        will work out
    e. Your knowledge and prestige because of more education
        than those asking advice

2. Which organizations seek out your advice?

3. (If an officer in a group): Is this group part of a larger organiza-
    tion? For example, are there other chapters in the city, the state,
    or the nation?
    YES_____   NO_____
    (IF YES) How is your group affiliated?

4. Does your organization have any of the following things?
    □ Intergroup meetings (meetings with other organizations)

☐ Meetings with public officials or important community repre-
    sentatives
☐ Meetings where someone from another neighborhood group
    speaks to your group or vice versa
☐ Joint meetings to plan how to accomplish a special goal
☐ Joint fund-raising activities

With all its ties to the larger suburb, Rolling Acres stands alone, proud of its uniqueness, its own resident newspaper and a "Rolling Acres Home Improvement Association," which stands ready to legally battle any resident not in compliance with stringent housing codes.

From an integral neighborhood

Sunday morning finds the local church filled with neighbors. "Others might call us 'the slum,' but we take care of our own," they say. "We all belonged to different [Protestant] churches, you know, but we all joined the [nondenominational neighborhood] church last year."

From a parochial neighborhood

Indeed, Rosegarden Homes had once organized to protect its right to privacy when a planned store was protested as potentially drawing in too many outsiders. Now that issue is dead, as is the last vestige of neighborhood organization. People we meet talk freely about national and statewide issues and Walter Cronkite is closer to them in many ways than their next-door neighbor.

From a diffuse neighborhood

As we turned into the Pembleton School District, a large moving van slowly maneuvered out from an intersection while its occupants tried to find the target home to disgorge its cumbersome load. We parked the car and began to walk through an area of temporary living quarters for innumerable white-collar personnel working at the nearby world headquarters of one of our country's largest auto companies.

From a stepping-stone neighborhood

"For Sale" signs dot the landscape with distressing regularity. As evening falls, we can smell the sweet and heavy odor of marijuana as teens begin their nightly ritual gathering under two neighborhood lampposts.

From a transitory neighborhood

Cyclone fences separate property lines. Or prickly rose bushes. Centered amidst the wire mesh of the fencing are license-plate-sized "Beware of dog" and "No trespassing" signs. Walking down the barren streets on a sunny afternoon, we can feel the steel-glare of neighbors peering out of a window—quickly darting behind their curtains as our eyes meet theirs. Even the Welcome Wagon lady admits great disappointment in her neighbors. "No one cares," she says.

From an anomic neighborhood

5 | Which Neighborhood Are You Talking About?

A. KNOWING WHICH NEIGHBORHOOD YOU ARE DEALING WITH

We have seen some of the dilemmas of individual neighborhood leadership and some of the processes that go on in the neighborhood. But now we must follow up on an earlier major theme we raised: What is the structure of a neighborhood as a human group? We want to turn to the idea of neighborhood as if it were a structure—as if it were something you build. Instead of first looking at what is going on inside this structure, here we are going to look at the shape of the structure itself. How is it put together?

Up to now social scientists who have looked at the role of neighborhoods, and practitioners of the art and science of changing neighborhoods have been locked into the traditional dichotomies of "strong" versus "weak" communities, "cohesive" versus "noncohesive," "organized" versus "disorganized" labels. These have been the bases for theories of juvenile delinquency,[1] studies of crime rates, and the design of such federal programs such as urban renewal,[2] Model Cities,[3] and the now-fashionable "community development."[4]

These efforts all rest on definitions of neighborhood. An implicit and often unconscious calculus exists whereby any given local neighborhood is measured against some ideal-type of what things were like in the "good old days" of neighborliness or the nostalgic and often distorted images of idyllic and charming traditional ethnic enclaves of our American cities in the earlier part of this century.

All of these stereotypes and myths about neighborhoods, as well as the more serious efforts at classification and descrip-

93

tion, seem out of touch with the reality of present-day urban neighborhoods. We must go beyond simple one-dimensional views of neighborhoods and use the tools of statistical analysis that go under the term of "multivariate analysis." Neighborhoods must be understood as multifaceted *social organizations*. And the variability in such structures is indeed impressive. In our research we have discovered neighborhoods that include the most formalized and hierarchically structured groups that might better be called miniature bureaucracies. In such settings people have fixed roles—they know who are the leaders and who are the followers, who specializes in fixing fences, and who can help when you are feeling depressed or have a sudden emergency illness or need someone to look after your house when you are gone.

In still other types of situations we have found neighborhoods to be nothing more than filling stations or stop-over points on the road of upward economic or social mobility. In many instances the neighborhood is sandwiched somewhere between the commuter's ride to work and the tavern or bowling alley or country club that is the central intersecting point of people's urban existence.

To understand better and describe the variety and highly specialized roles which neighborhoods can play in the lives of people, we have defined certain basic principles of organization. There are several things that are included: Do you identify with your neighborhood? Is there something to be involved in? Is there exchange? Is there organization? Is there contact? Is there a place for that contact? Does the neighborhood have any contact with the outside world—that is, does it have people in it that belong to other organizations? Does it have ways to get information about what is going on in the rest of the world? Does it have a rumor mill? These questions all boil down to probing three crucial dimensions:

1. Interaction: How often and with what number of neighbors do people visit and interact on the average during a period of one year?
2. Identity: How much do people feel they belong to a neighborhood and share a common destiny with others—a

sense of consciousness about what their neighborhood is and where it is spatially and symbolically?
3. Linkages: What channels exist in terms of both people with memberships in outside groups and those who bring news about the larger community back into the neighborhood?

Our research shows these three factors to be among the most critical ones for understanding how neighborhoods work and, therefore, the different situations that people find themselves in when they want to take action at the neighborhood level. Taken together these elements constitute the *social-structural* characteristics—differences in organization—which cut across social class, income, or ethnic lines in our society to define what neighborhood really is for people in urban areas.[5]

A Six-Fold Neighborhood Typology

Six basic types of neighborhoods are identified by creating a "high" and "low" score on each of the three underlying key dimensions. These represent the most frequently occurring forms which emerged from our field study.[6] Two additional types are logically possible but for several reasons they are more transient than the other six forms.[7] In chart 4 we show the characteristics of neighborhoods.

B. SOME OVERALL DESCRIPTIONS AND THE PERCEPTIONS OF RESIDENTS

(1) The Integral Neighborhood

This type of area is best described as "Janus-faced": It points in two directions at once. This means that people are really cohesive—they know each other, interact with each other, and belong to a lot of organizations, block clubs, and PTAs. It is a very active neighborhood. Its activities are both internal and external. People who belong to neighborhood groups also

Chart 4
Different Types of Neighborhoods

Type	Identity	Interaction	Linkages
Integral A cosmopolitan as well as a local center. Individuals are in close contact. They share many concerns. They participate in activities of the larger community.	+	+	+
Parochial A neighborhood having a strong ethnic identity or homogeneous character. Self-contained, independent of larger community. Has ways to screen out what does not conform to its own norms.	+	+	−
Diffuse Often homogeneous setting ranging from a new subdivision to an inner-city housing project. Has many things in common. However, there is no active internal life. Not tied into the larger community. Little local involvement with neighbors.	+	−	−
Stepping-Stone An active neighborhood. A game of "musical chairs." People participate in neighborhood activities *not* because they identify with the neighborhood but often to "get ahead" in a career or some other nonlocal point of destination.	−	+	+
Transitory A neighborhood where population change has been or is occurring. Often breaks up into little clusters of people—frequently "oldtimers" and newcomers are separated. Little collective action or organization takes place.	−	−	+

Chart 4
continued

Type	Identity	Interaction	Linkages
Anomic It's really a nonneighborhood. Highly atomized; no cohesion. Great social distance between people. No protective barriers to outside influences making it responsive to some outside change. It lacks the capacity to mobilize for common actions from within.	▬	▬	▬

belong to some groups that are not in the neighborhood. It is a kind of cosmopolitan neighborhood as well as a local center. This type of neighborhood can accomplish some rather unique things. When a problem comes up, it can reach out to various organizations. Moreover, it uses the authority and influence of particular residents to deal with problems quickly and effectively. This kind of neighborhood can also identify some local problem, such as garbage collection, get a group going and really take action.

By "integral" we mean that this community meshes with other institutions in the larger community. It has an effective base of organization and its people interact with each other a lot. Although it may have numerous internal organizations, the neighborhood reaches out beyond its boundaries into the broader community. It often is a neighborhood with a large number of professional people who are involved in community, business, political and civic work. They not only have a thorough knowledge of their neighborhood but also ready access to the social control agencies of the community. In a sense, the neighborhood and the larger bureaucratic structures are intermeshed, either through individuals or through neighborhood associations or other groups which belong to federations and can act on its behalf in a wider setting.

This neighborhood is both internally organized and externally linked. It is a rare and interesting neighborhood. One might argue that this is the ideal direction for urban neighborhoods to move in. Let us listen to the way people in several "integral" neighborhoods describe their experience:

[What things do you like best about living here?]

> It's a clean, quiet neighborhood. My office is in [local town] now so it's very convenient to my work. In my line of work I meet very many city residents with their problems and it's nice to live out here among them. Everyone in my neighborhood keeps his property up beautifully. [Male, 63]

> All the neighbors are nice people. I've been here so long it's almost a part of me now. My VFW post and everything is nice. [Male, 51]

> I can keep up with my children because everyone knows everyone. My neighbors are lovely people. [Female, 45]

> Neighbors are respectable. Those with children tried hard to educate their children. There are others who have developed good thriving businesses. They are concerned neighbors and dependable when one needs help. [Female, 58]

> One thing, we are close to our church and school. I know just about all the people in the neighborhood. [Male, 50]

> There is a certain neighborliness here. The neighbors protect each other or each other's property. [Male, 45]

[What would you need to know about the people moving in next door in order to 'size them up' as friends?]

> I would like to know about their religion or church affiliations. Their fraternal or sorority affiliates. [Male, 66]

> If they were friendly and like to communicate with others in the neighborhood and whether they would keep the property up. [Male, 27][8]

The Integral neighborhood may be one of the most important modern "inventions" of the urban environment. While we find it usually is easier for higher status groups to create, in fact it occurs in widely different settings. Here are three examples of its ubiquitous possibilities, excerpted from field ethnographers' notes:

A white-collar suburb:

> Most of the organizational structure is at the larger com-
> munity level, the city level, and it reaches down into
> the neighborhood. You can see it manifested in the
> neighborhood in that you can talk with people who are
> participants in organizations, churches, PTA. Some of
> them (like PTA, girl scouts, cub scouts) have local coun-
> terparts. They are part of a larger organization but they
> have an entity at the local level. But most of the organiza-
> tions are at the community level and they just have
> members who reside in the neighborhood. So in that
> sense it is not autonomous at all. I didn't find any organi-
> zations in the neighborhood that were exclusively
> neighborhood based. Ties in identification with the
> larger community are very great.[9]

An inner-city neighborhood:

> The school system has a reputation for having one of the
> very best elementary school areas and a very strong
> PTA. There are several community leaders, some of the
> key leaders of the whole city and just by virtue of the fact
> that they live there, appear to elevate status. There is
> definitely a positive reputation. It has a reputation out-
> side as the old area with a core of really good people and
> a fine school system. I got the sense that it was sort of
> looked to with the respect of an old area that had gone
> through a transition but was still in there. Some people I
> talked to—their parents used to live there and they had
> fond memories of it.[10]

A blue-collar industrial community:

> "Ford Park" is more like a small town—the people who
> were active in city-wide organizations lived in neighbor-
> hoods where people who were involved in local organ-
> izations were also neighbors. There were all these
> connections to various organizations that were local to
> "Ford Park," so people were involved in the same or-
> ganizations together. The neighborhoods were very im-
> portant to these organizations. There was more collec-
> tive scheduling, everybody was free from the factory.
> Their emphasis was on non-work activity, encouraging
> organizations, social clubs, and things like that.[11]

(2) The Parochial Neighborhood

In this kind of locale we have a version of the classic neighborhood about which we all have so much nostalgia. It has the sense of strong ethnic identity within the area, the sense of homogeneous values and culture, and the whole panorama of ideas that have traditionally been associated with the idealized cohesive local community or neighborhood. Because this is not a sectarian concept, parochial should be a small *p*. The direct connotation comes in the sense that this is a self-contained world.

This is a neighborhood that has values often counter to the larger community. It does not draw its values from outside. It is not a consumer of values as much as a producer of values. As such, it may appear to be deviant or out of line with major values of the society depending on what those values are. For example, it is not likely to be a locus of strong support for women's liberation, school busing, or liberal policies. Whatever happens to be the prevailing morality of the larger society is not directly absorbed by this kind of community. It may also be more "conventional" or "traditional" than the current value system of the larger society.

In relating to the larger world around it, the parochial neighborhood constructs a significant degree of insulation. Often this may be a linguistic kind of insulation. Or the insulation may be organizational in that it has a set of institutions which duplicate what is found in the larger community and, therefore, provides very effectively for the needs of the neighborhood without having to resort to the larger institutions of the society. In that sense this is a very contained community, and it tends to be very self-protective, able to screen or filter out values that do not conform to its own cultural system. Not only does it have a given set of values that are distinct; it also has a set of institutions which provide for the enforcement of those values.

The parochial neighborhood often has a basis of group identity which makes it much easier to develop this insularity. There has to be some sort of base—a heritage to draw upon. It could be racial, occupational, or generational: some common identity that has been associated with developing institutions to maintain a basic local commitment. Here is how people in some parochial neighborhoods describe their locale:

[What things do you like best about living here?]

> Our neighbors are friendly, kind, generous with their time. Helping with kids, giving of themselves when needed. It is kind of secluded down here, so we don't have door-to-door salesmen. [Male, 58]

> Like I said before, I like the large lots. That's why I came over here for, but not very much now. I like most of my neighbors, not all of them but most of them. Just about everything you need is close by, even the gas station. [Female, 49]

> Would you believe the atmosphere of the life in general? Neighbors' concern for each other which you do not find in a big city, it is close here. The neighbors have to be close to each other mainly because we are all black. You know I am not going to tell on my brother, we have to stick together. You know that's what they say about us anyway, that we want to tell on each other. [Male, 36]

Let us use one example of a suburban ethnic community. The fact that we describe it as "parochial" stems in part from the availability of local newspapers. Because they are in a foreign language rather than English, the newspapers serve two functions: They insulate at the same time that they provide internal communication. This kind of neighborhood often has one or both sorts of mechanisms—those that insulate as well as those that integrate internally. These mechanisms may be family systems, for example, or more formalized structures.

One example of a parochial neighborhood in our own research is the following locale at the edge of Detroit:

> This urban neighborhood has grown from a farming village to a carriage-and-trolley town and then to a white neighborhood in a black worker's city. Its fine system of social services, its hospital, and local city hall are all part of the larger city but retain a distinctly local character. It is an ethnic neighborhood where the stress is on being American. Its wealth relative to the rest of the city gives it some political leverage, but its populace is not

traditionally activist and feels exploited by the more intellectually liberal and active segments of the city. Many residents grew up in a provincial atmosphere of a small town without ever seeing the center of Detroit. In a city that survives in large part on welfare, these neighborhoods are fiercely independent even if eligible for aid.[12]

Class, race, age, and physical isolation all may be bases for the parochial character of a neighborhood. Clearly, the parochial neighborhood, once the dominant type, is less typical today.

(3) The Diffuse Neighborhood

Far more common than the parochial neighborhood is what we describe as the diffuse neighborhood. It tends to have the following characteristics: highly selective in its recruitment of residents, rather homogeneous setting (for example, subdivisions in suburban areas or public-housing projects in urban locations), and a situation where many families move in at about the same time.

However, and this is the critical point, what distinguishes the diffuse neighborhood from the parochial is that it has almost no active life of its own. Diffuse neighborhoods do have potential for a high degree of collective capacity to act, but they don't exercise it. As an example, consider a fairly affluent suburban neighborhood in which people are all middle-level management. If you go from door-to-door, you would find remarkably similar values and outlooks, but it simply exists—it hasn't been generated. It really isn't critical to the lifestyle and needs of the people that they act together with neighbors.

In the diffuse neighborhood, people achieve a degree of consensus without interaction. There is a common potential of sharing of values because of the shared homogeneity of background, so with a minimum amount of interaction, you can achieve a high degree of consensus. But news doesn't travel like wildfire because the internal communication structure is so limited that news may not travel at all. There is a paradox here. For example, our ethnographers found virtually all residents contacted in Rosegarden Homes spontaneously brought up the article on "privitism" which appeared in the newspaper a few days before. Their thinking is alike on many crucial issues. Along several blocks the backyard shrubs had died owing to the proximity of parking lots. Each neighbor complained. But none realized that their neighbors shared their concern until they were so informed by the ethnographers.

In a diffuse setting, people don't need the neighborhood, they don't depend on it for helping behaviors, and their own social networks are not focused in the neighborhood. There is great potential for the spreading of influence, but because there is not much interaction this may not happen. Here are some comments from residents of diffuse neighborhoods:

[What things do you like best about living here?]

> We don't have any trouble or disturbances in our area. I have a feeling of security here and I don't worry about people around. I feel relaxed here. Neighbors pretty much mind their own business. No parties or running around. [Female, 47]

> Take this neighborhood—we all have about the same amount of money, that's why we're in this same area. We are not bothered with a lot of hoodlums or distasteful types of people. It's a quiet, peaceful section. [Male, 49]

[What would you need to know about the people moving in next door in order to 'size them up' as friends?]

> You first have to know people before you could size them up as friends or not. Know more about them, their background, and how they treat people to know if they would be friends. [Male, 48]

> I would find what we have in common. If we liked the same things this would make it easier to be good neighbors. [Male, 25]

> As long as they live the same type of life [as mine] I don't care who moves in. [Male, 24]

We have seen through the eyes of residents that integral, parochial and diffuse neighborhoods are each distinctive, but share one feature: people have positive ties to their areas.

(4) The Stepping-Stone Neighborhood

On the other side, we have neighborhoods that have in common the fact that people don't identify with them but still perform various important functions within the neighborhood. This we call a stepping-stone neighborhood, marked by a paradoxically high degree of activism which continues even though there is a large turnover in residents. A typical stepping-stone neighborhood may have a large concentration of highly mobile, lower-level executives who come into the area, very quickly join all the organizations and become leaders of the neighborhood groups and then, two years later, move on so that these groups have to start all over again with new leaders. But these are talented, leadership-oriented people, often socialized to move very quickly from one neighborhood to another.

The pattern of organization in this neighborhood tends to be a little like musical chairs. There is a lot of turnover and a lot of new people coming in and out of the neighborhood and participating not because they have an ultimate commitment to the neighborhood but because they have an ultimate commitment to careers or to some other point of destination. Such neighborhoods institutionalize this kind of turnover and adapt well to the constant change in leadership. The Detroit community has a number of situations of this kind:

> The people like their neighborhood, but not too many stay. They usually move when the number of children becomes too large for the home. For these people, a larger home means a higher status. People move here to get away from integration in other parts of the city. The people in this neighborhood feel more a sense of belonging with their churches than they do with any neighborhood group.

People living in several stepping-stone neighborhoods sum it up as follows:

[What things do you like best about living here?]

> I like it because we have all paved streets and sidewalks and streetlights. It is what I call up to date for common, everyday working people. [Male, 55]

I want to get the hell out of here. Now you're gonna ask me why. Well, personally speaking, I don't like the neighborhood and I don't like the house and I want to live in a better neighborhood. [Male, 42]

[Why did you choose this neighborhood instead of some other one?]

To better our condition, where I was living the neighborhood was run down and the people were not concerned about their homes. [Female, 41]

It was a very good neighborhood a few years back. It was quiet, the houses were in much better condition than they are now. Some of the neighbors at that time were members of my faith so we just liked the area. [Female, 52]

I didn't choose it, we were having problems. The family service agency suggested that we get a better place to live and this is what they gave me. I didn't want a project because of raising the children. I had some trouble with the children in the old projects. [Female, 39]

[What would you need to know about the people moving in next door in order to 'size them up' as friends?]

If they were radicals or militants. Would want to know where they came from. One of my neighbors was a bootlegger. I don't want any more of that kind. I should want to know if they would be a good or bad influence on my daughter. [Female, 52]

I would like to know what neighborhood they came from and if they came from a bad neighborhood they wouldn't know how to act in a nice area. They would act just like they did where they moved from—drinking, partying, fighting and everything else. [Male, 69]

Stepping-stone neighborhoods are not found in only one social group. But they are what Vance Packard sees as the new living pattern of mobile, rootless Americans. Our town research shows this kind of neighborhood to be an increasing phenomenon—especially at the fringe of urban centers. One neighborhood staff observer put it this way in her report:

Temporariness is a paradox in a sense because, on the one hand, high status is shown by improving your home and, on the other hand, the people move out of these homes into which they've put so much status to higher status areas. Perhaps the way to move to a higher status area is to come from one that gives a reasonable amount of status in itself—or at least one in which the status criteria haven't changed in a while so it can be specifically, with reasonable accuracy, defined.[13]

(5) The Transitory Neighborhood

In the transitory neighborhood the population turnover is so great or the institutional fabric so divided that there is very little collective effort. The transitory neighborhood is pretty much what the word implies—a situation in-between. It often stays in this pattern for decades while successions of people move in and out. There are no institutions at all for dealing with this turnover. In contrast to the stepping-stone situation, where newcomers are immediately swallowed up by the organizations, the transitory-neighborhood turnover is either too great or the institutional fabric so restricted that there is very little activity and, if anything, it often breaks down into a series of cliques. These little clusters of people often have been there a long time; they belong to the same groups and never allow in newcomers.

Overall, the transitory neighborhood may show a moderate degree of participation, but this belies the fact that it is a divided system, usually with newcomers having low participation and oldtimers a high degree of participation. The result is a great deal of dissensus and lack of cohesion in the neighborhood. This is a neighborhood in which clique formation is very likely to emerge with little pockets of intense interaction. But on the whole, the level of interaction is not impressive. Here is an almost classic instance of the transitory neighborhood:

> Few neighbors are good friends. Usually they just say hello to each other and maintain most basic relationships. When asked why, most of them will reply that they or their neighbors just moved in or that they plan to move out of the area soon so that they did not have a chance or do not think it is worth it to start more intense relationships. The neighborhood is apparently of a transient, highly dynamic nature and most of the residents feel it is not worthy of a "larger social investment." The new-

comers are uncertain as to whether they are wanted and the old residents do not know how to "start talking" to new people, especially if they are black and "shy."

But, even the race is not to blame for the fact that somebody is new on the block. Sometimes people live together for years and do not know each other at all. Someone told me about a recent event to illustrate this phenomenon: one evening, inhabitants of a residential street could hear a woman screaming for help from a house and no one but a stranger, a black man who was passing by, answered her cries. Several minutes later he went up and down the street asking neighbors whether someone knew the woman and could stay with her in the house. To his surprise, no one admitted knowing and no one went in to help! (She had been living on that street for many years and she was white just as her neighbors were.) Hence, he went back and stayed with the woman until the ambulance came and took her and her husband (who was actually the cause of the panic) to a hospital.

This story really tells something about the lack of a neighborhood feeling or human interaction and about the almost paranoid fear and suspicion among people in the area.[14]

The norms of the neighborhood often suggest that one avoids participation in local entanglements either because the new families moving in tend to be different from oneself or because the very diversity of the neighborhood makes it difficult to feel any common set of values with one's neighbors. There may be cliques that operate in the neighborhood and small groups which may claim to represent the total neighborhood. Such subgroupings tend to be separate from one another and to form pockets of activity which are not really knit together as a total pattern of neighborhood cohesion. These are some comments from the people living in transitory neighborhoods:

[What things do you like best about living here?]

Twenty years ago this was one of the finest neighborhoods in Detroit. A great place to raise children. Nobody let their property go down. The lawns took second place to none. It was quiet and you could hear yourself think. It was close to my job. The memories we oldtimers share. Our plans and actions to restore some class to our declining homestead. It's still a little quiet here. Public transportation is still good as far as my employment is concerned. Mainly I like it because of the memories it holds. [Male, 58]

We sure are lucky. When the older folks move out we have been getting nice young couples. We don't have much in common but we still get along. [Male, 57]

[What things do you dislike about living here that might make you want to move?]

If I told you of 100 things I disliked, they would not add up to me making plans to move. Tried old friends, houses, and streets is all that comes to mind, and it's hard to dislike the elements which made you. We have problems like any other neighborhood, but the old timers look out for each other. [Male, 58]

I would like to get away from the city. I dislike project living.... I would like eventually to have a nicer, larger home on an acre of land. [Male, 48]

For one thing, we've sort of outgrown the home.... My husband doesn't like our neighbors very much but we decided to make an improvement rather than move right away. My neighbor who lives next door dislikes our children and dog and makes our life quite miserable. [Female, 36]

(6) The Anomic Neighborhood

We come now to the virtually "nonneighborhood". Anomic means individuated; people simply go their own ways. They don't belong to organizations, they may not see much of each other at all, and they have all the classic symptoms of the mass society. That is, the neighborhood is not a focal point of community.

The anomic neighborhood, because it's very highly individualized, doesn't have much of a leadership structure, so it is very hard to implement change through identification of key leaders. You won't get very far with that kind of strategy. But because it is literally "atomized," there is a lot of space between electrons or people. You can sometimes establish small ridges. At least there is space to move. You can begin very slowly to diffuse ideas or concerns. Since this is not a neighborhood that can protect itself from outside influences, it is very vulnerable in the sense that it has an open border. If you can reach one individual in that community at least you've got a foothold.

The Anomic neighborhood, because of its vulnerability to outside influence, should not be seen as a neighborhood which cannot respond to change. As a matter of fact, what people may not like about it is that it is unable to resist change.

The anomic neighborhood is not uniquely identified with the low-income area. It may cut across the social strata so that the suburban housing project or condominium area may be pretty anomic. We have to be careful with the stereotype that associates anomic with low-income black housing. The data suggest that it is not particularly black, nor particularly low income.

One anomic neighborhood in a prosperous and fast-growing suburb north of Detroit gives us a lasting recollection.

> Viewing the luxury condominium units within the shadow of one of the world's most glamorous shopping districts, it is difficult to imagine that this might be the repository of urban alienation often expected in less affluent neighborhoods. And yet the school district comprised almost wholly of the Alphaville Skyview Apartments is an anomic as any could be. We are struck by the stark contrast of the still smoldering red-brick structure serving as the local elementary school—burned and looted not two months after our first field visit to the neighborhood last summer.
>
> These are vivid images... of the "feel" of this neighborhood. We recall the brittle and suspicious glances and the unanswered greetings in response to "hello, pleasant day, isn't it?" Or the frequent replies to our expressed interest in "the kind of neighborhood this is to live in" with sharp: "Who are you? What do you want?"
>
> These are not distraught auto workers suffering the physical and psychological stresses of unemployment. These are people of all ages, many retired, supposedly "leading the good life."
>
> A few accept us in. And then our entrée is often

based upon knowledge of an occupant's relative. "Why," we ask, "is there such fear?" Answers are quick, short, and to the point—though accompanied by tea. "We don't like people nosing into our business. That TV program [a national TV program showing the 'swinging singles' in the buildings] made us look like some kind of licentious hotbed here." "Well, I don't know about the others— and, mind you, I don't care either—but *I'm* not that way!"

Now quickly Alphaville Skyview Apartments recede behind us as we swiftly cruise along one of Detroit's newest eight lane expressways headed directly south toward the east side riverfront of Detroit. Twenty minutes to readjust.

Beta Village is a neighborhood in inner-city Detroit adjacent to a long established upper class enclave. Charred, boarded up hulks suggest the preponderance of HUD owned, and presently unoccupied, four-flat residences. As symbolic a feature as any which assaults the eyes of a roaming observer is the corner store cleaners apartment. Now it stands, not merely abandoned, but a ready target of unknown missiles which have shattered and pocked its every window surface.

Stopping a postman to ask the meaning of a small orange-and-black sign displayed randomly in certain houses throughout the neighborhood, we met with the reply: "I don't know... that's not my block anyway." When asked the same question, two twelve-year-old youths gave two different answers. The one: "It's to tell kids they can ring the bell if kids are bothering them on the way to school or something." The other: "It's to show they don't want coloreds to move in."

Here are some comments from people living in Anomic areas:

[Why did you choose this neighborhood instead of some other one?]

Man, I could not find anything else at the time and it seemed to be quiet and peaceful here, but I sure was wrong. People have children running up and down the street all night long making all kinds of noises and it's hard for me to bring my children up to do the right thing. You know, to respect other people's property and to be quiet and to help keep a clean neighborhood. [Male, 38]

Truthfully it was the only house to buy for the price we could afford. We didn't actually choose the neighborhood, it was what we could afford. [Male, 24]

[What things do you dislike about living here that might make you want to move?]

The noise and the character of the people who live around here. You can't sleep; you might get a brick thrown in your window, bb guns shot in windows, they throw junk in your yard; and don't go telling them [parents] what their children did else they get mad. It's just a bad street to live on. [Male, 78]

Well, I tell you, as far as understanding, we have kids that break up bottles in your yard and pull down your telephone wires, but they live on the next street. They don't live here. [Male, 66]

Ah, the loss of hope that the overwhelming frustrations that might set in as a result of not being able to make my community a better place to live. [Male, 39]

[What things would you need to know about people moving in next door in order to 'size them up' as friends?]

I would not want to know anything. I don't care what kind of people they are just as long as they mind their own business. [Male, 24]

I don't care, as long as they take care of their business and I take care of mine. [Male, 58]

"Anomic" often means barriers between neighbors. In the anomic neighborhood, collective action is virtually impossible. Here's an example in one such area in relation to personal hostility and crime problems:

[There are] a lot of individual hassles over it [crime]. Their children get into fights or problems, after they clear it up the parents continue to feud. That is still on an individual basis. There is indication that when these feuds take place they are not really long-lasting permanent things.... The Joneses are on the black list this week, next week it might be the Smiths and the Joneses will be OK again.... The church has been robbed at least once.... They have five or six buses; they are constantly siphoned; windows are broken in the buses.... There is the neighborhood fence. Franks Bar and Lounge was robbed. The car wash is where they distribute the drugs; and then there is the one house that has been robbed three times and a couple other homes have been broken into.

There is a lot of crime there for such a small area. People talk about it, but they don't talk about it in terms of what shall we do about it; they just talk about it to note the fact. You get the feeling that people think "well it hasn't happened to me so I don't really give a damn. When it happens to me I will be concerned." We know at least one person that works closely with one of the detectives on the drug squad. She's worked with her family in her situation and her son. Her son is involved and she wants to deal with it. But you get this non-commital, non-involvement.[15]

Our research in the Detroit metropolitan area suggests that between one-quarter to one-third of all neighborhoods fall into the anomic pattern.

* * *

Each of the six neighborhood settings we have described can be seen as having some capacity either to facilitate, institute, or resist change. These settings should be seen as innovative: generating new values and norms, able to protect existing values and norms, or as being open to receiving new ideas or inputs. Depending on where your particular interests lie, you may or may not be unhappy about these types of neighborhoods; you may or may not feel it's good or bad to have this type of neighborhood. It depends again on whose values are at stake whether you're happy that you're dealing with a transitory or parochial neighborhood. Again, these have to be viewed as structural categories rather than value categories.

C. CONNECTIONS BETWEEN THE TYPES AND DEMOGRAPHIC CHARACTERISTICS

Much of the material dealing with neighborhoods has focused on spatial and physical characteristics.[16] While this is a useful beginning point, it has a number of pitfalls. First of all, physical proximity and social proximity are not highly correlated.

Being too close and crowded is not the way to insure social intimacy or identification. At the other extreme, it is clear that too little population or physical proximity is also bad for social cohesion. Either extreme of physical density is likely to have the same effect: It reduces the desire for and quality of social interaction.[17]

The neighborhood organizer must try to discover the social organization of a neighborhood and not merely to identify its physical attributes. Unfortunately, the way this has been most often approached by sociologists and other students of the subject has been via the social characteristics of its resident population as revealed in the U.S. census. How many people are affluent, how large are the homes, what is the average family size, what are the ethnic characteristics of the area, etc.? These are all important factors to consider in understanding the nature of a neighborhood. But the fact is that these characteristics may *cause* a neighborhood to develop a particular type of *social organization.*

We believe it is important to understand a basic difference between two processes that can shape a neighborhood: one is best described as a "selection" or "selective recruitment" process and the other can be called a "socialization" dynamic. In the first, the social characteristics of residents of a neighborhood are the result of voluntary choices people make about the kind of neighbors they prefer or the type of "lifestyle" they seek. Certainly, as income goes up and as ethnic and racial barriers fall, more people could be seen to choose a neighborhood among possible locations—perhaps taking into account factors such as the distance to work.

Socialization is a process in which neighbors influence one another over a period of time and shape the sense of community and values which then become the social norms of a neighborhood.

Both "selective recruitment" and "socialization" may go on to some degree, but we think that, more typically, people do cluster together in the same neighborhood for a host of economic and social reasons which are rather separate from the actual patterns of life in that locale. Having friends or relatives in a neighborhood may permit a person to anticipate what an area is like and to be drawn to it with a real "feel" for life in that setting. More often, families choose a given type of housing at a cost they perceive to be appropriate to them and in terms of convenience or shopping reasons. Only later is the neighborhood liable to become important as a social world. So we think it is best to see demographics as sifting and sorting newcomers to an area with a later dose of neighborhood values and "socialization" entering the picture.

This kind of urban "sifting and sorting" certainly is a major fact of life in the urban community. Both for good or ill, people have preferences, and the greater their affluence, the more likely we can assume that some form of "voluntarism" has gone into their choice of a neighborhood.

One more basic point is that when people select their neighborhood it may be with a great deal of knowledge about the demographics of the area—income, race, occupation, age, education, etc—but little awareness of what social organization really operates in that locale. Unless we assume that people with a certain income level, type of job, type of lifestyle, or racial identification always organize their local community in the same way, we must recognize that such demographic variables are "dependent" variables rather than "independent variables"—that is, they are the products of given kinds of neighborhoods, not its determinants. Clearly, it is not simply a one-way street. But research evidence points to the fact that persons within similar ethnic, social class, and related "homogeneous" strata do not live in monolithic settings. Much of the stereotyping of suburbs as sterile, homogeneous, and "wastelands" is a gross distortion.[18] Nearly one in three Americans now lives in a suburb, and this tends to banish one-third of our nation to the oblivion of bland conformity.

Our major point is this: social forms of neighborhoods are not determined by racial, social-class, or community factors alone—nor often in the main. Instead, great differentiation occurs *within* black neighborhoods, suburb subdivisions, and inner city enclaves. Thus we must treat two sets of neighborhood social characteristics: (1) the aggregate ones which depend on the kinds of people who reside in them, and (2) the organizational forms which arise or are developed.

Based on our research findings, several patterns link demographics with neighborhood social structure. First of all, integral neighborhoods can handle high population turnover. They also may have rather heterogeneous populations. This is not true of parochial neighborhoods which tend to be stable in population and to require a rather small turnover factor in order to maintain their integrity. Furthermore, such neighborhoods may have emerged under conditions of very selective in-movement—people who were of similar ethnic or cultural background. The parochial area does not require homogeneity of age or of family patterns. However, the value on privacy is high. If there are strongly shared values, then the self-contained and staunchly independent value system of the neighborhood can be perpetuated. Cultural, not demographic, similarity is the hallmark of the parochial neighborhood.

But for the diffuse neighborhood, homogeneity of demographic attributes seems to be the core element. Here, the fact that people are moving into a new subdivision at the same time, or having families at the same stage in the life cycle or in the same line of work might mark the basis of the typical diffuse neighborhood.

Clearly, the stepping-stone neighborhood can absorb newcomers—but perhaps even more basically it assumes the existence of its most "successful" leaders due often to upward mobility of its residents. Here, the fact of rapid turnover or the cycling of new cadres of leaders may be gradual. This can result in a clear schism in the locale—new values and lifestyles emerging which may clash with the older residents. Heterogeneity of status levels is frequently very pronounced. Privatism is not highly valued and a superficial sociability may be typical.

The high probability of a recent or continuing population shift is in the nature of the transitory neighborhood. However, even in the absence of such a factor, mutual aid has been replaced by the outside ties which newcomers retain and which old-time residents are excluded from. Heterogeneity of status may be very pronounced. Additionally, the failure of new leaders to emerge in the organizational context may weaken or lead to the absence of vigorous and active associational life in the neighborhood.

The anomic setting has little insulation from the outside and may typically be a very heterogeneous neighborhood. Individuals may be highly private in their responses, but this does not mean that the neighborhood as a whole is insulated from external intrusions—positive or negative. Individualism is more of a personal survival mechanism than a shared neighborhood norm.

D. SOME APPLICATIONS OF THE TYPOLOGY TO A SINGLE-PROBLEM FOCUS

Drawing upon examples of two contiguous, white, middle-class neighborhoods that we have studied, let us show how these two neighborhoods differ with regard to handling child-abuse cases. As both neighborhoods appear similar on demographic, socio-economic, and ecological dimensions (white, working-class populations of mixed age range, contiguously located in the older section of a suburban city), we must rely on other dimensions to explain the divergence in neighborhood response to child abuse problems: in particular, a description of the helping networks and social interaction settings of each neighborhood will be useful.

A Classic "Parochial" Neighborhood

The first neighborhood fits into our classification of a "parochial" neighborhood in terms of its homogeneity of values and culture. To illustrate the types of social interactions and helping networks associated with a "parochial" neighborhood, we have included the following excerpts from an ethnographer's field notes on this neighborhood:

Once you meet a neighbor, you are taken to other neighbors; momentum builds until groups are meeting with you, telling you: "we're different, and we're darned proud of it." When an appointment is made to speak with "some neighbors of yours," giving only three-quarters of an hour advance notice, and you arrive ready to apologize for the short notice, the door flings open with a group of people around a kitchen table laden with coffee and cookies, and apologies are given that 'only' eight neighbors could come.

Then come the neighborhood-based volunteer organizations, so many and so thick that at least eight families per square block are in some way touched by or direct participants in these organizations. What's going on in other neighborhoods doesn't really concern them. It's "taking care of our own" that permeates this neighborhood. All the emotional and physical needs are met within the community.

It tends to be very protective of its self-containment and has mechanisms that enable it to screen and filter out values that do not conform to its own cultural system. It was able, through its organizational networks, to mobilize its Catholic population to pay for protective legal pledges against busing when the Pope declared otherwise.

This is a neighborhood with high identity. Everyone loves it and even winning the lottery would not tear them away from the cohesion engendered within this neighborhood. More money means building on to the house, but never moving.[19]

In a parochial neighborhood such as the above example, we have hypothesized that the modal pattern would be an "indigenous" neighborhood; that is, neighbors acting as problem solvers, not just referral agents. The following field notes on child abuse in this neighborhood describe the indigenous resources utilized by the neighborhood residents in coping with this problem area:

Child abuse is cared for within the neighborhood— as everyone criss-crossing the organizational boundaries feels a sense of responsibility toward *all* neighborhood children and child abuse represents a clear breach of neighborhood norms. Since many of the neighborhood voluntary organizations deal with children as target populations, problems are recognized in early states. Children left out in the streets at 6:00 a.m. on cold winter mornings are brought into the homes of other parents: one takes responsibility for morning comforts, another gives hot lunches, and others attempt to talk with the parents. The community provides for its own! Even when a child is beaten, parents—closest in proximity—bound to a code permeating overlapping internal neighborhood networks—take it upon themselves to have a "neighborly" chat.

In the "Bucket Brigade," parents working on reading difficulties pinpoint unusual or abusive parent-child relationships during the child's story-telling time. The way this is handled is that: "we all get together and try to decide who to talk with. Sometimes it's the parents, and sometimes (if they know there might be repercussions on the child) we tell the school psychologist." Call the police? Bring in outsiders? Never! "We handle our own!"[20]

As can be seen from the foregoing excerpts, child-abuse cases in this "parochial" neighborhood would seldom reach the "officially reported" stage. Rather, the neighborhood would draw upon its vast reservoir of shared norms and values and upon its stable set of internal resources to cope with these problems within the neighborhood setting.

The Adjacent "Anomic" Neighborhood

The second neighborhood we will describe has been labeled an "anomic" neighborhood in that there is a marked absence of social organizations, patterns of participation, and a common identification with the local area or the larger society. The following excerpts are taken from field notes on this neighborhood:

Although people talk a long time with us, they do not see or talk to each other. They can't rely on one another for help. The values people have are not that much different from each other. On rare occasions where neighbors are induced to talk together with us, there is amazement that their concerns are mutual.[21]

Given that an "anomic" neighborhood is least likely to influence, mobilize, or alter the values of its residents through any form of resocialization, we should expect this neighborhood to handle its child-abuse cases quite differently from the methods utilized by the former "parochial" neighborhood. The modal pathway used by an "anomic" neighborhood is the "dependency-relationship" model. The following field note excerpts illustrate:

> Here a child abuse problem is simply dealt with. As the neighbors say: "Call the police—its not my kid." Or perhaps they call the elementary school principal. No attempt is made by neighbors to address the problem. The closest one comes to this is an actual court case where the family engaging in continued child abuse blamed and "threatened to get" the principal for having their child taken from their home. Here, if there is a problem "it's either call the police or wait until someone's dead or something."
>
> Also, once child abuse is cited, and the family finally does get plugged into the professional treatment system, there is total dependence. A "lock-in" model results wherein the *only* people that the family communicates with are the professionals—and the same neighborhood indifference exists, only to 'egg on' the abuser and perhaps provoke further abuse.[22]

Thus, we can see that in the "anomic" neighborhood child-abuse cases, if they are dealt with at all, are referred to resources external to the neighborhood. Reliance on external professional agencies can easily lead to an all-encompassing dependence on the part of clients, especially those who reside in an "anomic" neighborhood setting where there are *no* other ties to internal or external resources.

Problem Pathways and Child Abuse

We have discussed the set of decision and contact points that may occur in the context of a family-related problem. At this point, we are concerned with relating types of neighborhoods to the identification, treatment, and externalization of a problem. The critical processes implied determine the likely intensification or resolution of a problem such as child abuse before or after it has come to the attention of formal agencies of the community.

In the first stage—that of identification—contact with neighbors involves the nature of how the family sees its own behavior and how others define it—a self-other labeling process. In the integral neighborhood, visibility of all family behavior is likely to be high and deviant behavior from the norms of the neighborhood (which tend to coincide with those of the larger society) will be subject to some attempt at remediation or control. Here we are speaking of the probability that a neighbor will perceive a behavior pattern or will call it to the attention of others in the neighborhood. By contrast, the anomic neighborhood setting will be unlikely to have norms about "deviant" behavior or, if they do exist, the level of visibility will be low and no mechanisms for transmitting its meaning to others in the neighborhood will be present.

In the case of the parochial neighborhood, a great deal of the response in the identification phase will depend on what the norms about such matters as child rearing actually are. If they are consistent with the behavior noted by a neighbor, rejection will be low; if they are inconsistent, rejection will be similar to that within the integral neighborhood setting. In both the diffuse and stepping-stone neighborhoods, visibility and rejection will be moderate, but for different reasons. In the diffuse neighborhood, people interact relatively infrequently, although they often share common social values.

Recognition in the stepping-stone neighborhood is geared to who is active in organizations and who shares the values of the "joiners." Diversity within the neighborhood as to newcomers and oldtimers is not the key issue; rather it is the fact that organizations change members frequently and do not really take in all residents. In the case of the transitory neighborhood, the mechanisms of participation have declined and little opportunity for interaction occurs. Thus visibility is restricted to the most immediate neighbors or is uneven throughout the total area. Rejection of deviant behavior from larger societal norms is theoretically present but, in fact, is not mobilized.

E. SUMMING UP: THE TYPES ARE TOOLS

The typology we have discussed should be viewed as a useful tool rather than as a model against which everything should be compared. It is a way to organize and include some complexity which has been ignored previously by social scientists and practitioners in social agencies. If it is not helpful, there is no reason to invest in it, intellectually or otherwise, unless you are just interested in dealing with abstract models of neighborhoods. Likewise, if the scheme is any good, it should not only be applied to suburban or central city areas, but it should cover the gambit irrespective of ecological location.

Too often in sociology we tend to create rigid categories. If the parochial neighborhood persists in being parochial over a long period of time, there is a lot going on to insure this. In other words, to produce stability there has to be a lot of maintenance. That means some new structures if the old ones no longer perform. If they do generate new structures that can serve the same insulating functions, the parochial neighborhood will persist. But we cannot assume just because we have labeled them that they are fixed.

Each of these local community settings can be seen as having some capacity to facilitate, resist, or institute change. In some cases they are innovative and generate new values and norms; in other cases they are able to protect the existing values and norms; in still additional situations they are able to receive new ideas and influences.

The neighborhood types we have described must be viewed in structural rather than value categories. Each has a different potential with respect to change; each has the capacity to generate its own institutional processes. In the research to date we see these as dynamic processes rather than fixed structures. A diffuse neighborhood can evolve into a parochial neighborhood and the integral neighborhood can emerge from a former stepping-stone. What are the dynamics of this process?

One of the questions to be looked at by any social group thinking about its own future and its own interests is how much it wants to invest in geography. They may be locked too much into geography, whereas other groups are less spacially tied. The link between geography and power undergoes change. As geography shifts its significance, it is necessary to make a judgment—either as a policymaker or someone interested in pursuing a particular goal—as to whether you are relying too much or not enough on geography to achieve a given social value.

Our discussion has focused on the capacity of a variety of neighborhoods to generate problem coping structures. To what extent can the solutions, or at least reasonable alternatives to problem solutions, be found in the larger society? Whether this is psychiatric treatment, soothsaying, or exorcism—which may get more popular—does the neighborhood have a system of helping, and if so, how good is that system? The systems of helping that emerge in different neighborhoods may be complementary to or competitive with those systems that have been developed in more formalized parts of the society.

Neighborhoods must be looked upon as dynamic in both structure and process terms. But structure and content have to be related in order to understand this. We find that there are certain kinds of people ("neighborhood exploiters") who really know how to use the helping network of the neighborhood. They do not hesitate to borrow a cup of sugar and several other things as well. A certain cultural norm would look upon this situation of helping as an indicator of humanistic values, a sense of trust in others and willingness to relate to all those things is expressed symbolically through exchanging "gifts." Another cultural group may find that attitude rather offensive in that people should stay to themselves unless it is an emergency. There are some cultural differences in the utilization of the neighborhood. To assume that everyone has to be a part of this network is not the case.

The interest of social scientists in the concept of community should go beyond the operational steps of defining what is neighborhood or community. Moreover, it would be very pretentious to say that any typology could define the entire nature of neighborhoods in urban areas. We have selected a certain part of reality and locked into that particular slice of it. Yet, the richness and variety of neighborhoods and the impact they can generate strongly refutes a model which sees only the individual in a relationship with the larger structure. A critical link between an individual and society is the neighborhood. The "middle levels" of social strcuture such as local community are very political and pivotal—the source of much that may eventually filter down to the individual from the "mass society."

Organizer's Exercises
Chapter 5

TYPING YOUR NEIGHBORHOOD

The Three Dimensions:

1. Identification:
   - ☐ People feel they have a great deal in common
   - ☐ People give a name to the area
   - ☐ People plan to stay in the area

2. Interaction:
   - ☐ People visit with nearby neighbors at least once a week
   - ☐ People meet in organizations or social groups—not necessarily in the neighborhood but with neighbors
   - ☐ People see others in the neighborhood as getting together often even if that's not their own pattern

3. Linkages:
   - ☐ People belong to a lot of organizations outside of their neighborhood
   - ☐ People know about someone who is a community leader or has "connections"
   - ☐ People see others as having "connections" if not they themselves

   There are three chances to say "yes" on each dimension. Go over each of your answers. Then pick out the "strongest" dimension. In which one of these characteristics is your neighborhood strongest? Perhaps a good rule of thumb is that if you can't answer at least two of the three examples as "yes," then your neighborhood is really not strong on this attribute.

Several years ago Sister Jo began a systematic action of organizing block clubs. She went door to door and talked to people about the necessity of organizing block clubs and having greater communication among neighbors. At present, there are 18 block clubs and most of them were organized at her or Father Jim's instigation. The youngest block club was organized on Heyden Street on July 10, gathering more than 50% of the households (representatives) at the first meeting.

From a Catholic inner-city
neighborhood

Last year we heard of a developer's plans to turn the 15 acres behind us into high-rise apartments instead of single-family homes. We got on the phone to friends [in the planning department at city hall] and our lawyer friend. We sat down and hashed out the basic argument to fight the high rises. Then we got a few neighbors on this block to help phone everyone in the [elementary school] district announcing a meeting at the [local elementary] school. The planners and lawyers spoke and when they left we wrote up petitions and decided to send letters to council members and the mayor. We sure snowed the council with the number of our people that showed up at their meetings.

From an upper middle-class
neighborhood

6 | The Neighborhood Activist Role:
Domestic Policy on Home Turf

We have seen that each neighborhood type has a different structure of leadership. We have noted that the general principles of organizational leadership (i.e., that there are two levels, both formal and informal) implies that the kind of role that the activist person plays is going to be very different depending on the neighborhood setting in which he or she functions.

In considering these different structures of neighborhood, we immediately find ourselves asking the question, What is it that the activist or the community leader actually does? Very often, this is a matter of looking at the flow of influence or information that occurs in the neighborhood. Therefore, in addition to the structure of the neighborhood, we also have to talk about the *process* of influence that goes on there.

A. NEIGHBORHOOD PROCESS: THE FLOW OF IDEAS AND INFORMATION

News derived from the electronic media, word-of-mouth, and ideas from community people outside the neighborhood form the lifeblood of conversations and personal influence in a neighborhood. A number of years ago, researchers looking at voting behavior concluded that most of us make up our mind who to vote for, not because of the direct appeals of given candidates or their slogans alone—but always in combination with the immediate social contacts and "significant

125

others" with whom we interact. This so-called two-step flow of communication often works as part of the neighborhood information system.

In Chart 5 we have schematically defined how each type of neighborhood is in reality an "information-processing center"—either keeping information out, filtering its content, or providing various "interpreters" to help an individual evaluate what the news means.[1]

The lines forming the neighborhood rectangle reflect the information barrier—if it is solid this is because people identify with the neighborhood and see it as "inside" versus "outside" world; or if not solid, how permeable is the "wall" membrane of the neighborhood. Arrows coming into the neighborhood from the top consist of mass-media information—TV, radio, newspapers—and the contacts with leaders and influential people "in the know." The arrow going across inside each neighborhood is the diffusing of opinions due to the number of "opinion leaders" in the neighborhood—it measures the spread of rumor as well as news dealing with subjects such as energy conservation, societal values, and civic, state, and national problems. The arrow pointing up or down between the mass media and key influentials inputs to the neighborhood is based on measuring the amount of time that people in each neighborhood take to absorb the opinions of others versus give back or talk back either to the media or to key influentials or others outside the neighborhood.

Now let us look at each pattern. In the integral neighborhood there is a complex flow of information into and out of the setting. People do listen to the media but do not rely on its direct-information input. A great deal of "comparative shopping" goes on in this neighborhood—where the message is checked against other reliable sources such as key influentials in the outer community or opinion leaders within the neighborhood itself. In addition, the integral neighborhood "talks back" to the outside world—it doesn't simply absorb ideas, it generates them. We have called this pattern an "information-exchange system."

Chart 5
Neighborhood Information Processing

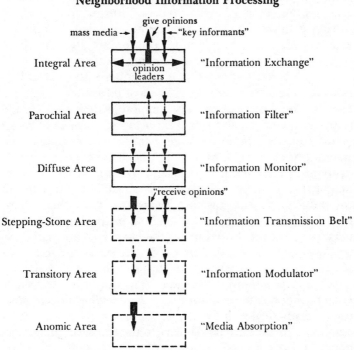

The parochial neighborhood is set up with one major function for its information system: to keep ideas and values out that go against the norms of the neighborhood. Failing this, the job of the local opinion leader is to keep in touch but then to "translate" rather than simply "transmit" information from the outside. The secure boundary to unwanted intrusion by the mass media is maintained by low individual listening and viewing compared to other neighbors and by the vigilance of neighbors who serve as "counterpropaganda" agents. "Information filtering" is the label for this pattern.

The diffuse neighborhood has no strong barriers against outside information although it does have some contacts with key community people and does not simply soak in information uncritically. Overall, however, the system of information processing is relatively weak, and at best the diffuse neighborhood is a "monitor" of various types of information—perhaps storing it but not using it to take action—neither resisting values or ideas that are alien nor reinforcing them. We have called this an "information-monitoring" pattern.

Our research shows that the stepping-stone neighborhood is a great consumer of all kinds of information—people have a wide variety of friends, opinion leaders, and "inside dopesters" and are also relatively heavy consumers of mass-media content. The information net is thus cast wide in the stepping-stone neighborhood. At the same time it is not a deep information-evaluation system. What is shared between neighbors may be relatively trivial and nonserious in content—sports and fashion discussion more than "hard news." But one thing is clear: people in the stepping-stone neighborhood are "wired in" to the latest fads and can drop glib comments at cocktail or office parties as needed. This pattern we may describe as the "transmission-belt" process.

The system-of-information flow in the transitory neighborhood is more absorbing than reacting. People must use media to deal with problems that once were dealt with by neighbors. If they are newcomers to the transitory neighborhood there are just a few trusted or valuable opinion leaders that a person can count on; so old friends and outside sources must be kept in touch with or else isolation and information deprivation is the result. The need to seek information is high in the transitory neighborhood but the structure for providing it is inadequate. "Information modulation" is the process which occurs.

The dangers of the "mass society"—where individuals are manipulated by subliminal advertising or become ready adherents to mass totalitarian causes—have always seemed a distorted or exaggerated picture of modern society. And yet in the anomic neighborhood we have the prototypical setting for such processes to achieve a frightening reality. Our research shows that people in these residential settings are the highest consumers of mass media—watch more hours of television per day and use advice and information from media more than from friends or neighbors or community groups. Overall, the anomic neighborhood has no "radiation belt" of protection from media manipulation—its lack of opinion filters provides no way to "check-out" rumors or mass media appeals.[2] This pattern is described as "media absorption".

Making Use of Influence Pathways in Neighborhoods

Knowledge of the "information network" and how it works is an indispensable tool for the person taking action in their local neighborhood. Often it is by seeking to make effective inputs into that "information flow" or by counteracting its effects that efforts of an energetic citizen-activist are crowned with success. Sheer dedication, energy, and will power may not overcome the inertia or barriers that are built into neighborhood information systems.

We think we can suggest some ways in which the findings of this analysis can be related to efforts at changing attitudes about given external events or seeking to intervene in the information-processing system used by individuals. Considering each neighborhood setting in terms of a "message response" pattern, important differences between locales can be described.

We can now explore some suggestions about information flow related to the neighborhood types.

Integral Neighborhood

Information flows into the area from many sources and is also quickly passed around from resident to resident. This means that the neighborhood is usually "tuned in" to what is happening beyond its boundaries and that generally people do not resist accepting the views of outside institutions. If newspapers indicate there is an energy crisis, people in the integral neighborhood will relay that perspective to others and will not have to spell out what that means. Lack of alienation from Washington may help. If there is a change in attitude by government, people in the integral neighborhood will quickly shift their behavior—or even more likely be the first to try to validate what is given out in media messages. They will do so by checking with their "inside sources" and personal contacts. If the message proves wrong, it may have a hard time getting another hearing.

A critical acceptance means not just automatic conformity to what a health agency, city hall, or other broadcasting institutions communicate. Therefore, it is very important to encourage some feedback on messages—to permit people to use their various critical "check out" channels. Giving a balanced picture of both sides of an argument is a necessity. Very one-sided appeals will get rejected in the integral neighborhood, and the future willingness to "hear" your message may be diminished.

Using a combination of personal and media inputs is highly recommended: put out a flyer or newsletter but also make sure that those people who are distributing your message really can back it up with additional information. In turn, use such disseminators of your messages as feedback agents to modify or improve the program or idea you have put forth. There is a really competitive information process going on in the integral neighborhood and you must make your case in a high-traffic environment. People will tune you out if you are too biased in your approach or did not treat the message receivers as knowledgeable and desiring of participation in the process of action and communication.

The Parochial Neighborhood

Here the communication process is characterized by parsimony—few words but a common frame of reference. People will not easily pay attention to your message unless it is put across initially in local terms. For example, if you are interested in school curriculum change, don't focus on ideological terms such as "traditional" versus "progressive" theories. Instead, use a language that you find people in this kind of neighborhood are using themselves.

People in the parochial setting are very wary of media slogans and may be very slow to respond to appeals that suggest rapid social change or "modernity." If it is possible to bring an idea into discussion in a way which conforms as much as possible to what already is valued, that concept will be most likely to be responded to. Once the message is "translated" into local terms you will not have to keep repeating it: local social acceptance will be linked to reinforcement of people's actions. So it is the initial "opening up of the dialogue" which is the key task of communication in this setting.

The Diffuse Neighborhood

Because this kind of area has a low volume of information flow, the basic communication problem is generating excitment or interest that will motivate people to tell neighbors or to feel the message applies to them. Let us take the instance of parents being concerned about the safety of children walking home from school. Since residents seldom interact, the scope of this problem may not be recognized. Even though many parents are concerned, they are not aware of how widespread is the fear. This "pluralistic ignorance" greatly reduces the response to a problem. Since opinion leaders are neither common nor widely used, only if people see written complaints or read about how many other parents are concerned might they be willing to add their voice to an effort at taking action. Until that "critical mass" is formed, people will not act. And once a recognition of a problem occurs, consistent followup is necessary to keep the communication channel active.

The need to "reinforce" the initial message is important in the diffuse neighborhood. It means that even where individuals have each found a useful part of the answer to a problem, the integrating of these elements is far from automatic. Because people have been adamant in support of an action in the past, it cannot be assumed they will be "tuned in" on the latest "news" and local need.

Stepping-Stone Neighborhood

People in this setting are very much "tuned in" to the latest mass-media fads and fashions and will respond quickly to a message couched in terms of "new" or "latest." The sensitive antennae of residents means that using newsletters or even electronic mass media is a cheap and effective way to get a message across. At the same time the "quality" of messages may suffer so that those which require new behaviors may be harder to get across than those requiring readily visible attitude or external behavior change. For example, getting people to sign a petition advocating a change in local utility rates to encourage conservation may be in tune with the "right" attitude. And if buying small cars is part of that message, neighbors in the stepping-stone area will readily see what others are doing in response to that message. But when the mass media suggests the energy crisis is "over," then car size may rapidly increase once again.

Little in the way of long-term behavior change can be assumed to originate from the influence of neighbor behavior, but a great deal of reinforcement of media norms is likely. Communicators in this kind of setting must use a style which is rapid and contemporary—the medium may indeed be the message. Packaging is critical; timeliness as well; intensity and intimacy of content are secondary.

Transitory Neighborhood

The communication process here is tied into small cliques and to the reliance on old friends or other confidants. There is no general "grape vine" that will relay a message. If it once existed, it does not work as well now—especially for new residents. The communicator can't rely on shared norms and must instead go out to various parts of the neighborhood and cover all of the diverse settings where people carry out their day-to-day responsibilities. Reaching people via their workplace, through the school, or by means of checking group membership lists may provide the channel to get your message across.

One example pertains to a black neighborhood of older persons. Many with medical problems rely on their children who live in other neighborhoods or who are away at college or universities. Their higher educational level and the sacrifice of older parents and grandparents has permitted these younger kin to serve as "outside experts." If a hospital or clinic wanted to insure that medical appointments or medicine regimens are maintained by these older residents of the transitory neighborhood, it might be effective to send a mailed card to known children or grandchildren, not just to the designated patient. This reinforcement via external link means that neighborhood communication occurs, but through the indirect role of residents' nonneighborhood social ties.

The Anomic Neighborhood

Information—whether it originates within the neighborhood or is packaged in a TV story or newspaper article—simply will not make the rounds in this kind of neighborhood. The absence of the "grape vine" is based on the fact that people see little in common with their neighbors. Even if they do go to them for emergencies or to get help, they do it reluctantly and with no high expectations that they will be better informed or helped.

The isolation of the anomic neighborhood may lead those residents with economic or family resources to simply ignore what is said or done in the neighborhood. In some instances we find that parents instruct their children not to play with neighboring children because of the fear that the bad name or simply cold shoulder they will receive is a good reason to avoid rather than contact neighbors. Where the low income individual is simply unable to get out of the neighborhood setting, they may find their resources serve more to show the futility of breaking out of the world in which they are locked.

Yet communication from the outside does not encounter the barriers that can be erected by the parochial neighborhood setting with its "sifting and sorting" of nonconforming information. While people in both the stepping-stone neighborhood and the anomic setting are receptive and reliant on mass-media sources of information, in the latter case lack of contact with neighbors coupled with an unwillingness to act on the information received may reduce the neighborhood resident to a kind of passive member of an audience.

Many messages will get sent to the anomic neighborhood from a single information source, but the reinforcement in terms of action or any attitude change cannot be enhanced by using other available channels. Each message must either be constructed just for a given "campaign" or the level of influence sought reduced to the repetition of slogans or one-sided propaganda efforts. For example, getting parents to accept a new curriculum change may be done only via repeated notes sent back with the children or a series of newsletter announcements. Little direct personal influence followup will occur since few opinion leaders exist. Thus, only a direct one-to-one persuasion effort can be used to supplement the mass-media approach. Without this intensive and costly effort, messages will fade easily. The more complex the problem, the more difficult the task of communicating. Reinforcement must be direct and aimed at each isolated household.

B. LEADERSHIP ROLES IN DIFFERENT NEIGHBORHOOD SETTINGS: ADDITIONAL KEYS TO ORGANIZING STRATEGIES

Another dimension of the influence process in neighborhoods is the role patterns of individual activists. Drawing upon information from 400 interviews provides a means to examine how the "reputational" or informal activist functions in a variety of settings.[3] Let us first examine some responses regarding self-perceived roles. The particular question asked is: "How about your own role in community activities.... Which do you do most? Which comes next?"

Answers were divided according to two "styles" of leadership as first discussed in chapter 3. The first of these is usually labeled "task" or "instrumental." It refers to the emphasis upon the leader providing specific goals and setting out what the group should do. In contrast is the "expressive" or "social-emotional" style of leadership. This is a leader role emphasizing the pulling together of different elements of a group, the developing of smooth relationships among members and a generally cohesive building approach to leadership. Each of the two "styles" can be effective, and there is in fact extensive literature on the functioning of small groups stressing that both types must be present to have effective "group process." There are times when one approach is needed, and an inflexible approach using either style is less desirable than a blending or developing of both. Seldom can the same person act in both styles, so a variety of styles usually means more than one leader is active in the group.

Both integral and parochial neighborhood activists stand out distinctly from those in other kinds of neighborhoods: They are heavily task oriented. When second-choice responses are added to the analysis, activists in integral neighborhoods maintain their "task"-role emphases, but a sharp change is found for activists in the parochial setting: They become "expressive" leaders. The same trend exists in other neighborhoods, but not to the same degree.

Several patterns emerge from the study. Integral neighborhoods are associated with many activists playing an exclusively "task-oriented" leadership role. Both transitory and anomic neighborhoods have relatively high percentages of activists who play an exclusively "task" role. In all neighborhoods the typical pattern is for activists to play both a "task" and a "social-emotional" role. This dual role pattern is especially pronounced in parochial, diffuse, and stepping-stone neighborhoods.

Activists in integral and parochial neighborhoods indicate that political action reasons such as "speaking and acting on issues" or "keeping the peace" provide satisfactions in their roles. Those in diffuse, transitory, and anomic neighborhoods stress the "social-contact" reasons. Activists in stepping-stone neighborhoods emphasize "linkage to the community" reasons such as "getting more information on the (larger) community" and "community improvement." Activists in both transitory and anomic neighborhoods mention political-action reasons for satisfaction less than their counterparts in other neighborhoods.

If we consider both "community" and "social-contact" motivations of activists, the "protective" role of the activist in parochial settings stands out. Since respondents could indicate more than one reason for satisfaction with the activist role, the multiple basis of such leadership patterns is of interest. In anomic areas, one out of five activists had more than one type of satisfaction. In diffuse, parochial, and transitory, more than one type of role satisfaction was indicated by a majority of activists.

Links between Formal and Informal Neighborhood Leadership

A major consideration in the understanding of the reputational neighborhood activist is the degree of "system" character to their functioning. In other words, are they really a strata of leaders—a structural component of the neighborhood—or merely a disparate, highly individualized group of isolated actors? The answer which are data provides suggests this varies with the neighborhood type.

Multiple nominations of the same activists are most common in parochial, stepping-stone and integral neighborhoods. They are roughly half as frequent in diffuse, transitory, and anomic areas. Activists in integral neighborhoods know another activist in better than four out of five cases; this drops to only one out of two in parochial, diffuse, and anomic neighborhoods.

High levels of integration of the "activist network" occur on both indicators only in the integral neighborhood. Diffuse and anomic neighborhoods show consistently low coherence of their activist structures. Parochial, stepping-stone, and transitory have one of the two indicators reflecting high levels of organization among their activists.

The linkage between the formal and informal leadership structures of a neighborhood is a vital factor in the organizational life of any locale. Let us now explore several facets of this relationship. First, the question of formal leadership. Here we are referring to voluntary associations and the significant roles which neighborhood residents play in such organizations. In the base study we asked each respondent: "Have you ever held an office or position of leadership" in a series of groups listed as the compendium of different types of voluntary associations, such as PTAs, block clubs, church group, professional associations and other organizations.[4]

Once again, the type of neighborhood revealed rather wide differences in the proportion of respondents indicating they were or had been active in a formal organization role. Thus, only one in five respondents from anomic neighborhoods reported such participation, compared to more than two out of five persons in parochial neighborhoods. Integral neighborhoods ranked a close second with 39 percent, transitory was only slightly above the low set by anomic neighborhoods—23 percent reported being active as formal leaders.

Given the variability in holding a formal leadership role, what about the "reputational" activists? How likely are they to simultaneously serve as formal leaders? In parochial neighborhoods we find the close overlap between formal and informal leadership structures; 93 percent of people regarded as leaders in the area report they have been or are leaders in formal groups. Neighborhood "reputational" activists in stepping-stone and anomic settings are least likely to report also being formal leaders. Yet overall, more than three out of four reputational activists have at some time or another also been in a leadership role in a voluntary association.

C. ACTIVISTS' TACTICS: SOME PATTERNS TO KEEP IN MIND

Let us now examine specific tactics that are most frequently used by neighborhood activists. In our Detroit area studies, we discussed fifteen specific kinds of actions. These range from such direct confrontation tactics as a march on city hall to informative actions such as pamphlet writing. In analyzing the efforts of activists we have divided these into two kinds— "organizing" and "action." In the former category are such things as "door-to-door canvassing," telephone campaigns, pamphlet writing, and "mobilizing for political purposes." In the latter group are a range of specific tactics such as writing to public officials, boycotting, presenting demands to officials, calling for a resignation, calling in outside people, writing letters to the editor, or placing ads in a newspaper.

The four "organizing" strategies may generally be thought of as steps preceding subsequent influence attempts on city hall or other intruding or relevant external institutions. Most activists use more than one tactic—particularly in stepping-stone and parochial neighborhoods. Much activist work may be limited to efforts at organizing. This is especially so in transitory and diffuse neighborhoods. If we rank the frequency with which each of the "organizing" and "action" tactics are used by activists in one type of neighborhood versus another, some important patterns come to light.

Activists in stepping-stone and parochial neighborhoods have the first or second highest "scores"—in seven out of fifteen listed tactics. Both also stress "actions" over "organizing," especially the stepping-stone area. These patterns imply that "action" capacities are highly developed in the two areas. By contrast, activists in the transitory neighborhood are

Chart 6
Special "Styles" of Activists:
Actions and Strategies

(First ranked by neighborhood type)

	Organizing Actions	Influence Actions
Integral	Telephone Campaign	Letters to officials
Parochial	Pamphlet writing	Letters to editors, negotiations
Diffuse	Mobilizing for political purposes	—
Stepping Stone	Door-to-door canvassing	Leaders presenting demands, ads in newspaper, picketing, or boycotting
Transitory	Door-to-door canvassing	March on city hall
Anomic	—	Calling in outside party

preoccupied with "organizing." Apparently seeking to retain or regain past effectiveness requires this kind of emphasis. In both integral and diffuse neighborhoods activists scope in terms of tactics is not as extensive as many other kinds of neighborhoods. In anomic neighborhoods, only two kinds of "action" strategies are typically used by activists.

If we focus on a description of what is unique to the style of the activist in different neighborhood contexts, each of the six variations has its own configuration. We find that in the integral setting, telephone campaigning and letter writing to officials are efforts which are highly unique. For the parochial neighborhood it is a combination of pamphlet writing and the dual-action tactics of letters to the editor and negotiating with some individual or institution.

The stepping-stone neighborhood has three different kinds of action tactics which are most frequently employed: (1) leaders presenting demands; (2) ads in newspapers; and

(3) direct action such as picketing and boycotting. On the organizing side, activists in stepping-stone and transitory neighborhoods use door-to-door canvassing more than do activists in other neighborhoods. In terms of "action" efforts, the march on city hall occurs most often in the transitory setting.

Two kinds of neighborhoods had only a single distinct tactic: For diffuse neighborhoods it is the "political mobilization" effort and for anomic areas it is calling in an outside party to deal with an issue (see Chart 6).

A Closing Word

The patterns of informal activist tactics we found in the various kinds of neighborhoods are useful guides to what is a typical, feasible, or promising basis of action. Clearly, a combination of "trial-and-error" or "scatter-gun" or "seat-of-the-pants (or skirt)" approach may be employed to advantage. But we think it is important to place action strategies in some context—a background of expectations in order to evaluate or to set goals for action. Knowing what others have used can avoid "reinventing the wheel." This goes on far too frequently and is time consuming and demoralizing.

By sharing with you what we have found in our neighborhood studies you may be able to devote energy and inventive genius to the second task of the neighborhood organizer—relating to outside individuals and groups. There are some guiding results of our research here as well. Let us now shift our focus on the neighborhood activist to that very crucial job.

One lady has a pretty strong image to begin with. When they instituted the bucket brigade throughout the city, she sort of headed that up. She consults with mothers in other neighborhoods. She told us she didn't think she had made any progress and then the teacher had called her over later in the year and said that her scores had improved and she was really pleased with herself. I understood that in some areas teachers didn't like the idea of parents coming in but in this city it's not like that at all. Teachers can see somebody coming in and upsurping their role by saying I don't have any training at all and I can teach kids to read just as well if not better than you can.

From a blue-collar suburban neighborhood

One woman organized a fund-raising thing for the school where they got Krogers to supply a meal, and they made $500. This was uninitiated, too. They came to Ferguson and said, "Could you use some money for the library?" He said, "Of course," and they went out and did this. It wasn't PTA; it was just some people in the neighborhood. They put on a luncheon. The Icarian Club raises money and sends it back for hospitals.

From a white-collar neighborhood

7 | **The Bridging Role of the Neighborhood Activist**

Being a neighborhood organizer or activist can be very schizophrenic experience. By this we simply mean that efforts to build local cohesion and to move ahead with specific goals often clash. This is true in some kinds of neighborhoods more than others. But in general what underlies both activist tasks is a "brokerage" function. Sometimes it's carried on between different groups *within* the neighborhood. Often it is a "foreign-policy" challenge. In this chapter research findings and their implications will be knitted together as a design for organizing in different neighborhoods.

The link between formal and informal neighborhood leadership is seldom automatic. But once the bridge is built, it permits the neighborhood to reach across its internal boundaries and to extend unified links to outside groups. We measured this process in our Detroit area research by asking informal leaders whether "people, groups, or organizations come to you for advice on issues or actions?"

With the exception of the low positive responses in integral neighborhoods, activists in other locales show a similar pattern: somewhat less than half report they are asked to help organizations. Two is the *number* of organizations on the average that an activist "serves" when playing an advisory role. Thus, although relatively few activists (one out of four) act in such roles in integral neighborhoods, on the average each one serves 4.3 organizations. This is close to twice the average of other neighborhoods. By contrast, when an activist is an advisor to organizations in the parochial neighborhood he has relatively few "clients"—1.9 on the average.

Does the advisory role of the "reputational" leader serve to link the neighborhood to other outside voluntary associations or merely to coordinate and aid local groups? The answer is that important variations occur by neighborhood type. Not surprisingly, in the parochial context informal leaders serve mainly to advise in neighborhood organizations; both in the integral and transitory neighborhoods they mainly advise nonneighborhood, "external" organizations. In this sense they serve to link the local area to the larger community structure. Such leaders in stepping-stone and anomic areas also play this role but to a lesser extent. Chart 7 provides a pictorial summary of informal leader roles in their "inside"-versus-"outside" linking roles.

Neighborhood Types and the Linkage to Voluntary Associations outside the Neighborhood

We have discussed a number of ways in which information is processed in different kinds of neighborhoods, some of the key roles that activists can play according to the type of neighborhood, as well as hints on the different patterns of neighborhood. Now we must investigate what the relationship is between each neighborhood type and the foreign-policy perspective on outside organizations. What are some of the patterns that emerge which describe the particular style of internal-neighborhood-versus-outside-organization ties?

Let's start with the integral neighborhood. Here, almost by its very definition, the neighborhood itself as well as the activist in it have a dual role. They serve to build local cohesion as well as to tie the members of the neighborhood to outside resources. In this sense there is a two-way flow of influence and often the activist in the local neighborhood is an officer in a voluntary association outside of the neighborhood.

First, its activists provide leadership resources to community-wide groups. Secondly, the members from the neighborhood are an important resource in staffing and providing the backbone of many community groups. In turn, the neighborhood receives an up-to-date systematic intelligence

Chart 7
Neighborhood Type and Activist-
Linkage Roles

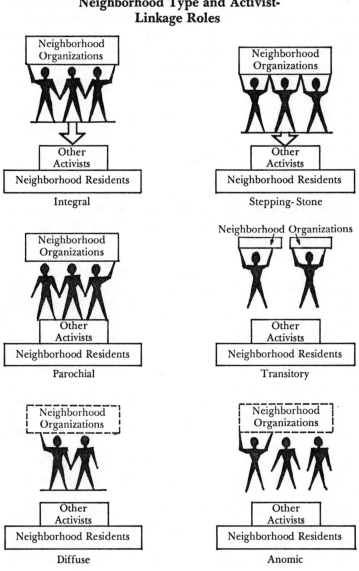

Integral

Stepping-Stone

Parochial

Transitory

Diffuse

Anomic

on what is occurring in the rest of the community, as well as learning valuable tricks of the trade in techniques for effectively organizing and carrying out its goals. There is clearly an elaborate two-way street of foreign policy exchanges. We call this pattern in the integral neighborhood "grass-roots outreach," which means that essentially there is a capacity at all levels of the neighborhood to draw on whatever resources lie outside of it.

In contrast, the parochial neighborhood is characterized by what we call "insulated linkage." That is, the role of the activist tends to be one in which outside organizations are to some extent foreign territory. The activist may be put in a situation of real role conflict if he or she serves simultaneously as an officer in an outside group and as a neighborhood activist. This is the kind of role inconsistency that we spoke about in a general sense earlier, and it is most likely to occur in the parochial neighborhood.

At the same time, this is a type of neighborhood setting which does not stress formal activism. The residents are very self-contained and stress privatism. Their contribution to outside organizations is minimal. Therefore, the lines of linkage both from membership as well as leadership of outside groups to the parochial neighborhood is a very tenuous one. In turn, the way the activist and the residents relate to outside organizations is one of a minimal tie, often based on very indirect forms of influence.

Let us now turn to the diffuse neighborhood. Here we find that the pattern of outside ties which is most typical is that of cross fertilization. In this kind of setting, the members of community groups provide almost the only basis of activism occurring in this local neighborhood. Their role as neighborhood activists is often dependent upon their experience and participation in a community group. The cross fertilization involves the fact that the neighborhood gains by the activist being involved in outside organizations. In turn, the activist brings to outside associations concerns and input about the neighborhood that would otherwise not be available to the outer community because residents themselves tend to be relatively low participators in the larger community, and when they do participate it is as individuals and not through more systematic ties.

At the same time, it is relatively unusual for the activist in the diffuse neighborhood to play a leadership role in outside associations. This is much more likely to occur in the integral neighborhood.

Turning now to the stepping-stone setting, we find a pattern which we call "elite integration." In this context, the core of highly active individuals in the neighborhood consists of a circulating elite who are also active as officers and leaders of outside groups. In this sense, the outside organizations are the ultimate destination and reference point for these neighborhood activists. Their loyalty to the neighborhood is really a secondary one, and, in this sense, the likelihood is that the values that they will bring the neighborhood will be the values of the larger community organizations. It would be almost impossible for a conflict of interests to arise between these two entities—the local neighborhood and the community association.

In a stepping-stone neighborhood, almost as soon as a person becomes a neighborhood activist, he or she is connected to a circle of outside community organizations. All too often, the budding leader is lost to the neighborhood as a resource.

In turn, as the rotation continues, new individuals moving into the neighborhood will often have ties to outside groups or will be seeking to make those ties as part of their social-mobility pattern. The result is a circulation of groups at the top and relatively limited grass-roots-membership contact between outside groups and residents of the neighborhood. But it must be kept in mind that the stepping-stone neighborhood is likely to have as intense and complex a set of organizational links between itself and the outside community as does the integral neighborhood. In fact, it may be even more complicated in the stepping-stone setting because the neighborhood will tend to consume from the outside association network, while at the same time producing the same values. In the integral neighborhood it is more or less a matter of generating influences that impact upon the larger associational network of the community.

In the case of the transitory neighborhood, we find the greatest danger and likelihood of co-optation of the activist. This is true for two reasons. First of all, the neighborhood itself has a split among its residents in terms of newcomers and oldtimers or in terms of values. It generally has organizations which may have flourished in the past but which have fallen into a state of decay. One consequence of this situation is that leaders or officers of community-wide groups may take over the shells of such organizations, breathe new life into them, and as a result become active in the neighborhood. This kind of outside manipulation of the neighborhood is a very great danger to the transitory neighborhood. Unlike the stepping-stone area, it becomes very difficult for this neighborhood to regenerate its leadership cadre. The turnover in the transitory area is of a somewhat different character than that of the stepping-stone area. There may be very many talented individuals who come into the transitory neighborhood and who want to remake it, but the barriers which exist in the neighborhood, the lines of special interests between existing groups, the selective recruiting processes of the older organizations make it difficult for newcomers to break in.

A good illustration of the dynamics of leadership in a transitory area can be seen in what happened to a local community in a resort area of the state of Michigan. Over a period of time this community experienced a tremendous influx by urbanites escaping racial, crime, and pollution problems by fleeing to the more serene and environmentally-pure locale of nearby Lake Michigan. Over the years, as more and more of these individuals have moved in to the community, there has been a gradual change in the values of the neighborhood. The traditional local organizations—Kiwanis, Lions, Elks— have declined as new light industrial and small corporate elites have moved in with their own special professional associations and organizational linkage. The effect of this has been a decline of the traditional civic groups and the increasing influence of outsiders. As each new outsider moves into the neighborhood, he seeks to protect the environment by trying to restrict others from following suit. The result is that the individuals gradually take over the leadership structure of the community, while the locals withdraw and become less active.

The problem of the transitory neighborhood is one of stimulating a new foreign policy built around protecting a local culture and at the same time importing those things which are considered necessary from the outside. It is indeed a difficult and challenging dilemma.

Finally we turn to the anomic neighborhood, and here we find an almost total lack of effective relationship to the community at large. Leaders of outside organizations may reside in such neighborhoods, but are very seldom active in them. There is no linkage between outside organizations and the neighborhood through its leadership structure.

In general the anomic neighborhood has a low proportion of active people in organizations. Where it is able to draw on such outside resources, the neighborhood's disunity and apathy frustrate the effectiveness and significance of such outside expertise. Overall, the anomic neighborhood tends to provide a kind of absorption of outside expertise without generating any internal resources of its own.

Foreign Policy in Light of Neighborhood Type

Let us now provide some suggested tactics and remedies for each of the six neighborhood types as these relate to the external community. These basic strategies are graphically illustrated in Chart 8.

In the case of the integral neighborhood it can afford to interact with power-elite groups and to use strategies of direct linkage with bureaucracy. Because it has a wide variety of

Chart 8
Typical Neighborhood Relationship Linkages

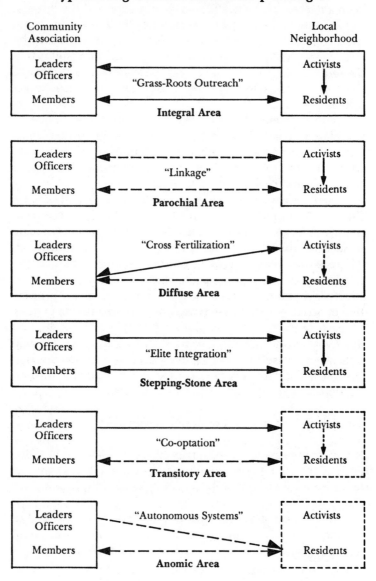

avenues of contact it can check and counter the tactics which could be detrimental if city hall or another outside agency is involved. Here we have a variety of residents who have a well-established commitment to their neighborhood and who are experienced in dealing with the external world. This tends to eliminate the problem of conflict of interest for activists as well as reducing marginality from the neighborhood for those who take on outside groups as adversaries. Many different residents can serve as a "grass-roots" leader or representatives in relating to outside groups.

The parochial neighborhood is often limited in the number of its activists who feel at ease relating too closely with outside agencies. In such a setting tactics which use *indirect links* to bureaucracy should be emphasized. The danger of co-optation is not great but a lack of "common language" and interaction skills where its activists feel "outside their element" could mean a failure to protect neighborhood concerns and values. Working closely with a relatively small cadre of highly experienced activists may be a necessary approach.

In the case of the diffuse neighborhood, local activists are few and far between. Much of the life of the neighborhood is symbolic and actual experience in relating to outside groups may be even less well developed than in the parochial setting. Development of leadership skills is the primary task of the organizer. For these reasons it is a good idea to place limited responsibility on as many residents as possible having memberships or contact with outside groups. This spreads the responsibility for foreign policy, making it possible to see who emerges as most effective via a natural sifting and sorting around specific tactics and problems. Thus, if one person turns out to know about local zoning ordinances or to have fought a battle with city hall over a personal problem of their own, it may be very effective to bring her/him to a small meeting so that others may learn directly about mobilization or collective action. The "common sense of community" and the facilitating of interaction among neighbors may well be all that is needed to build the basis of neighborhood foreign policy. Even if a nonresident needs to be drawn in to show local activists how to mobilize and respond to outside groups, this is preferable to untutored locals.

In the stepping-stone neighborhood the danger of co-optation due to the low neighborhood identification of its leaders is greater than in almost any other setting. For this reason every precaution should be taken not to recruit someone into a major foreign policy role who does not at the same time communicate with and train an apprentice to take over the role in case they leave the neighborhood. The danger of co-optation of leaders in stepping-stone neighborhoods suggests a clear need for accountability of actions to neighborhood residents. One way to help this occur is to get leaders to identify publicly with neighborhood causes and to avoid the use of private negotiations with outside agencies or organizations. The stepping-stone neighborhood usually has an abundance of activists so the organizer can pick and choose the right person to carry out foreign policy tasks.

In the transitory neighborhood there is so little base of local cohesion and collective action that leaders or activists must end up depending heavily on other organizations for guidance and resources. While this, of course, further weakens the local autonomy of the area and increases the co-optation syndrome, it cannot be avoided. The result: There is no new generation of local leaders and no effort to knit together the remnants of groups which exist among different elements of the neighborhood. Newcomers particularly are lost in the transitory neighborhood, and if a special effort is made to tap their expertise and organizational *savoire faire*, the result enhances the capacity of collective action on problems. Since the oldtimers to the area are probably the most loyal to the area—having remained despite population change and the weakening of local organizations—their advice and interest when sought out and brought to the attention of the new active resident can be a good strategy for action. The primary role of the neighborhood organizer is to create an "internal" linkage which emphasizes the building of indigenous human resources with a realistic reliance on outside linkages. Foreign policy for the transitory neighborhood means the acceptance of co-optation of leaders while at the same time building the critical mass of local leadership skills and personnel to make this pay off. This is accomplished by extracting *quid pro quos* for the neighborhood as often as possible.

For the anomic neighborhood, the primary job of the organizer is to increase the utilization of outside organizational resources and to reduce its characteristic isolation. The objective is not worrying over the danger of co-optation as much as it is a matter of focusing attention of outside organizations and elites—as well as apathetic local residents—on the problems and needs of the neighborhood. While many residents use local resources, this is less because of their effectiveness than because people in the neighborhood do not know or cannot reach other resources of problem coping. A primary task is to open up channels of cooperative action with other neighborhood groups and then to borrow outside resources until the confidence and skill has been developed locally to carry out effective leader efforts.

Activist Role Differentiation: Summary Exploration

We have identified a number of role relations, action patterns, and tactics which seem to be preferred in a given type of neighborhood by the individual who is identified by their neighbors as a person active in getting things done. In addition, the flow of information in various types of neighborhoods has been examined. Now we can look at how activism can be effective by using the characteristics of neighborhoods as conditioning factors for success or failure.

We start with the *integral neighborhood.* Here, activists are best seen as a large group relative to the population, who are linked to one another, and who stand midway between local formal associations and external organizations. They are very task oriented. Political action is a major part of their activities. They have generally a lengthy tenure in their role. While local groups may be in close working ties on occasion, they are a rather distinctive strata whose major function is linkage with external groups. They generally do not use militant direct-action tactics and are relatively less visible in the neighborhood compared to the elaborate associational structure of the neighborhood. Rather than being constantly active they are a stable feature of the neighborhood's leadership structure.

One major task of the leader/organizer in the integral neighborhood is to carry messages from local residents to outside organizations and back again. In providing this "feedback" to the outside, it is possible for activists to influence a host of external organizations: to heighten sensitivity to the concerns of people in their neighborhoods.

These "linking persons" have a real power base when one considers that they are not only organized themselves, but they can also get their message across to many other groups. Indirectly, they can exert power in that they can get other organizations to act consistently with their own goals, without actually taking over those organizations and without the necessity of setting up every type of organization in their own neighborhood.

In parochial neighborhoods, activists are also a relatively tight-knit strata but mesh much more directly with local groups than is the case in other neighborhoods. They are very often officers of groups and provide a highly visible part of the leadership structure of the neighborhood. They can be mobilized quickly and use a wide arsenal of action tactics. They serve less as transmission lines to external groups than as translators of local interests—more often advising local groups than outside organizations. They are task oriented but also shift to more expressive and "social emotional" roles—a highly versatile set of individuals.

In the parochial neighborhood, information—whether on health, news, or other significant events—seldom passes directly into the neighborhood. Whatever information does get through is filtered and modified by key opinion leaders. These individuals usually have very strong commitments to the neighborhood, and they are not as likely to express to their neighborhood the interests of the larger community. On the contrary, they are more likely to express the neighborhood's concerns.

One major obligation of the activist in the parochial neighborhood is to protect the neighborhood against outside influences that are not consistent with the neighborhood norms while, at the same time, communicating to residents what the outside world is doing.

In *diffuse neighborhoods,* the reputational activist is a relatively autonomous leader with links to the external community and a motivation based on the satisfactions of having many social contacts. In linking to outside groups they are more the transmitters of local action efforts than the successful organizers of collective action. Given the small organizational structure of the neighborhood, they must seek to create the basis of collective response but often fail to obtain a stage of "action."

They are individuals who often may have to lead in ways that are "social emotional." But they also can use some distinctive action tactics. To a larger extent, they are "ahead" of their neighbors rather than expressing their will. What actions they take often may reflect their own priorities and interests in linkage with other groups rather than the expression of effective neighborhood organization.

One major characteristic of the diffuse neighborhood is that even though there is a commitment to the local area, people don't really have to express it in concrete behaviors. What we find here is an attitudinal commitment. Thus, people identify with the neighborhood because they find it a pleasant place to live; they know that, in general, their neighbors share their lifestyle. Most important, however, is that there is no critical dependency on the neighborhood as a basis for shaping or protecting that lifestyle.

In this situation, information often flows very slowly with the result that people may perceive higher agreement on issues than may, in fact, exist. Consequently, the neighborhood is often relatively slow in taking action when threatened because there isn't much contact and relatively little organization, even though there is a great deal of organizational potential. A problem is how to galvanize the neighborhood into taking action. Once this has occurred, the neighborhood often finds a new sense of solidarity and increased interaction. However, this new-found activism usually subsides back to its normal level. Thus, only under conditions of crisis or threat does this neighborhood become organizationally active, the latent potential for increased interaction being ever present.

The activist in the diffuse neighborhood is often someone who finds her or his greatest satisfaction in working with outside groups and only secondly is able to carry messages to many people in the neighborhood. To some extent, a few residents may call upon the activist to accomplish something but often those activities do not get very far. This suggests that where there is a lack in diffusion of information, the activist almost has to go to each household to make individual contact. This is a situation where an outside agency may have to put in more resources than planned, for too often when that agency relies upon mass media the results are disappointing.

The *stepping-stone neighborhood* is not the most typical kind of area but is of particular interest owing to a seeming paradox. Somewhat like the integral neighborhood in its degree of internal organization that is matched by the outward focus character of many of its residents, the population itself presents a different profile. The pattern of mobility generally stems from the many individuals who move in to be close to their place of occupation but who are called upon to move again—either up the ladder or laterally—as soon as the organization or corporation changes its needs. In many respects, this neighborhood develops certain capacities to deal with this population change.

In this kind of neighborhood, people are very active in outside organizations, but the unique characteristic of this situation is that the person who is a neighborhood activist tends to achieve this role subordinate to his participation in larger community groups. Thus, if he is an officer in an outside group, and he moves into the neighborhood, that can quickly lead to his becoming a neighborhood activist. This kind of neighborhood leader does not provide the two-way interaction we see in the integral neighborhood. Instead, there is the importation of leadership skills from outside organizations. To that extent, the activist in the neighborhood really has a direct relationship with outside organizations that is more important than his role of activist in the neighborhood. In the stepping-stone neighborhood, the activist is often in training to become a member of a community elite. He/she uses the activist role as a reinforcement of that elite status.

For stepping-stone neighborhoods, in keeping with the dynamic character of this kind of setting, many action tactics may be tried; a willingness to engage in direct confrontation is not lacking. Although the neighborhood may have a high turnover of such leaders, it appears that activists are a highly "renewable" leadership resource. They are a coherent strata and are highly motivated to play their catalytic roles. Primarily "social-emotional" in leadership style, they use tactics which bring them in contact with newcomers as well as old-time residents. Yet they also have many ties to outside organizations. In a number of ways they serve as a strong force for expressing the needs and interests of the neighborhood vis-à-vis external organizations and to those who have a less involved organizational life but are local residents.

In *transitory neighborhoods,* the population turnover is so great or the institutional fabric so restricted that there is very little activity. The neighborhood often breaks down into a series of little clusters of people. Some have been there for quite a long time; they belong to the same groups and never allow newcomers to come in.

Newcomers tend to have low participation; oldtimers have high participation. The result is a great deal of dissensus and a lack of cohesion. The norms of the neighborhood often suggest that one avoids participation in local entanglements either because the new families moving in tend to be different from one's own or because the very diversity of the neighborhood makes it difficult to feel any common set of values with one's neighbors. There may be cliques that operate in the neighborhood—small groups that participate very highly and some of which may claim to represent the total neighborhood.

The absence or decline of local autonomy in the transitory neighborhood means that activists and local groups are often dominated by people who are members of outside groups and who have literally taken over the neighborhood leadership function. Those who had been active at some time in the past may no longer have a constituency and may simply stop serving in a representational role.

In transitory neighborhoods the primary challenge to activists is to broaden neighborhood organization. Under conditions of population turnover or clique formation, highly diverse sets of individuals tend to exert pressure on outside organizations often with highly individualized and competitive tactics and goals. Too often, activists in the transitory neighborhood are lone entrepreneurs who can be militant and effective in expressing neighborhood concerns but on behalf of a constituency that is sometimes more historical than current, more a nucleus than a cross section of the neighborhood.

In *anomic neighborhoods*, we find virtually no leadership structure. Whatever linkage occurs with outside organizations does not really flow through any neighborhood activist system. Groups which may even meet in the neighborhood do not really tie into any neighborhood identity. Therefore, the leadership as such and the role of the activist cannot be described as anything more than the obligations and tasks that an individual might take on as a single resident, or perhaps as a representative of some group that they belong to in the community. There are no meaningful constituencies for the person who is active, and there is no real cohesion to the structure of influence.

Individuals may choose to live in the anomic neighborhood in order to have the kind of anonymity that they consider necessary for their own lifestyle. But the fact remains that whether it is partly voluntary or a condition of certain more affluent areas, the anomic neighborhood cannot readily mobilize to respond to common interests.

This, therefore, is not an area that can produce solutions to problems and it may have serious difficulty in even being a consumer of anything more than the most superficial of mass-media messages. Opinion leaders, the local activists who can be relied upon, and the kind of personal filtering of information that is found in other neighborhoods will simply be lacking in this kind of social setting.

When there are activists in anomic neighborhoods, they tend to be heavily "expressive" in their leadership style. These individuals work very much on their own and are not a coherent strata of leadership. Motivated to be involved with outside community groups they are important links to the larger institutional network. Given the limited local organization and the difficulty of generating collective action, they are less frequently active and have a rather restricted repertoire of tactics. These individuals are often "old hands" at their role— persistent dabblers in issues—sought out as advisors yet really lacking in a genuine power base.

Do It Yourself: The Activism "Game"[1]

Perhaps you have already been comparing your own neighborhood to these we have described. It may well be that you are one of the kinds of local leaders we have described. Or, perhaps, you have thought about mobilizing your neighbors and have wondered where to begin. There are certainly a wide variety of organizations and individuals whose understanding of the neighborhood settings to which they relate could help them to be effective—whether they are school administrators, professionals in a human service organization, police officers, parents, or simply people who are fed up with city hall and want their neighbors to "get it together."

Perhaps the actual situation you may find yourself in as an activist does not exactly fit the models of neighborhood we have described. Why don't we begin by taking some of the

Chart 9
Organizer's Exercises
How to be an Effective Neighborhood Strategist

Diagnosing the Neighborhood		Newsletter	Door-to-Door

For Each of these Characteristics Indicate if it is True of Your Neighborhood:

			Newsletter	Door-to-Door
1.	During the year do people in the neighborhood get together quite often? (Interaction)	YES	✔	NO
2.	Are there many people of different backgrounds, lifestyles, or social levels who live in the neighborhood? (Heterogeneity)	YES	✔	✚
3.	Do people in the neighborhood feel they have a great deal in common? (Identification)	YES	✚	✔
4.	When someone has something on his mind that is bothering him, are neighbors willing to help? (Social-emotional support)	YES	✔	✔
5.	Do people in the neighborhood place more value on their family privacy than on being in touch with neighbors? (Privatism)	YES	NO	NO
6.	If a bill collector came around asking about a neighbor, would people in your neighborhood refuse to give out any information? (Boundary maintenance)	YES	✔	✚
7.	Do many people in the neighborhood keep active in groups outside of the local area? (Linkage)	YES	✔	NO
8.	Are there many people who move in and out of your neighborhood? (Turnover)	YES	✚	✔

Chart 9
(continued)

Taking Action

Mass Media	Key Local People	Organiza- tion Lists	New Grass-Roots Group	Random- Sample Survey	Pipeline to City Hall
NO	✚	✔	✔	NO	✔
NO	✔	✔	NO	✔	NO
✔	NO	✔	✔	NO	✔
✔	NO	NO	NO	✔	✚
✚	✔	✔	NO	NO	NO
NO	✔	NO	✔	NO	NO
✔	✔	✚	✔	✔	✔
✔	NO	NO	✔	✔	✔

KEY: ✚ = best first action
 ✔ = effective follow-up action
 NO = not cost-effective action

more basic characteristics of neighborhoods we have found to be pivotal for organizational action and change. In Chart 9, we have listed eight of these: social interaction, identification, supportive helping, privatism, linkages to the larger community, boundary roles, status heterogeneity, and resident turnover.

We have also picked eight frequently employed action strategies of local leaders. These include: use of a newsletter, door-to-door contacts, newspaper and TV ads, using a group of key active people, drawing on people listed in organizations who live in the neighborhood, starting up a grass-roots group, conducting a cross-section survey, and getting city hall to have a representative work with the neighborhood.

Now here is the way to devise your own strategies and decide where to go first and what to do that is most likely to be productive. For each characteristic of your neighborhood that is listed, look across at what type of action is the optimal one to employ. We have grouped strategies into three kinds; (a) those which are the best first step; (b) those which can be fairly effective as follow-up actions; and (c) those which are so costly in time and effort that it doesn't really make sense to use them. We have indicated the first type with a "plus" sign, the second type is indicated by a check mark, and the third by the word "no."

Let us try out this matrix of neighborhood activist choices. Suppose the neighborhood in which you are functioning is one where people are in frequent contact with one another. The most efficient first step is to use a few key people and try to mobilize them. They, in turn, will pass the word on and serve as diffusors of your action or message. Newsletters, door-to-door contact, and paying for media ads are all most costly and time consuming. They might work, but they are not "cost efficient." Developing a new local group is certainly a useful follow-up action and the idea of a city hall person being in close touch with the group would also work in this neighborhood as another follow-up action.

Now, let's deal with a neighborhood that is heterogeneous. Because people are different in their social patterns it is hard to find a "language" for a newsletter or a format that will catch the eye of many kinds of individuals. Educational levels and misperception of the intended message may occur. A boomerang effect can set in. So both newsletter and media ads are only moderately useful—perhaps as follow-up actions. But what can be done first? Our answer is that door-to-door canvassing and wide coverage using personal contact is the only effective first action to take. In this way, many people left off of organizing lists known by some people, or "key influentials" suggested by others, can be contacted and, perhaps, drawn into the effort you are developing.

Suppose a neighborhood has very little going for it except that people all like it there and feel a certain common sense of identity. What is a good first step in neighborhood action? In this case we have indicated that a newsletter can be a very effective start. If people share many things in common and are not usually in contact with one another, the newsletter can serve as a catalyst and a way to inform even the newest resident about things occurring in the neighborhood. Since people have a positive orientation to the neighborhood, they may readily go on to take other steps—form a group, contact people in organizations that already exist but are not focused on neighborhood problems—or conduct door-to-door campaigns that were first mentioned in the newsletter.

If a neighborhood has many individuals who are sympathetic listeners but there is no other formal leadership, we have indicated in Chart 9 that the best first step is trying to get some help from city hall. The problem is that help with individual problems does not provide the expertise for dealing with issues like zoning, city service efficiency, getting more funds for special projects, protection against environmental threats, and the like. These "task" leadership skills may be developed eventually but, in the meantime, a pipeline to city hall can be a good holding action.

When a neighborhood has a strong emphasis on the privacy of the family and household, it is often hard to develop a base for collective action. Chart 9 indicates that one effective first step is the use of mass-media ads or appeals. This may be very useful as we have noted in the case of the anomic neighborhood, if it is then followed up with efforts to mobilize people who belong to community groups that live in the neighborhood. In turn, a door-to-door campaign, while very time consuming and expensive, might have some success as a follow-up action. Trying to reach a few key people can also be helpful.

The neighborhood which has a rather impermeable boundary—perhaps due to language, values, or other insulating qualities—often has greater strength in resisting change than in anticipating problems that may affect the neighborhood. In this situation, a good first strategy for the local activistic effort is the direct personal contact approach—a door-to-door canvassing. Without some initial ice-breaking step, the individual may find other steps met with resistance and subversion, particularly if the activist is not one of the long-term residents. Getting in touch with key influentials in the neighborhood and developing a local grass-roots group may prove effective as follow-up actions.

Where the neighborhood has a large number of "joiners" in it who have many ties to outside groups, then the job of the activist is often to draw upon lists of community groups and reach people via their organizational affiliations. This is often more effective than any newsletter or similar technique. It also means that if there is a problem involving city hall, some of those "joiners" have contacts that can be used to get information or to direct local action. It would be redundant and inefficient to try to establish such a pipeline on your own.

For the neighborhood characterized by a high turnover of residents, the problems of the activist are often overwhelming and lead to a great sense of futility. We suggest that a good initial tactic to utilize in this situation is the newsletter. It provides newcomers with some idea of what is going on in the area and also serves to remind long-term residents that the neighborhood still is a place with stability and continuity. Where the personal information-flow system has broken down, the newsletter can often serve as the information exchange around problems of families needing help in fixing up their homes, child care, or other mutual aid that people do not easily find available in their area. Setting up a new grassroots group made up of both newcomers and oldtimers is a good follow-up tactic. So is the use of media ads in a local newspaper or circulars at local stores or the police and school facilities in the area. The main job of the activist is to establish communication links and then try to use other methods to "institutionalize" them.

A Closing Caveat

The concept of a neighborhood activist is clearly one of leadership for specified efforts on behalf of a given issue or problem. Like the diverse theories of delinquency which have surfaced over the decades, we may exaggerate one dimension of an individual's behavior—implying that the labeled delinquent has this single role as the constant behavior pattern. Is the "rap" deserved or based on past or brief "glories"? So we may err in seeing the activist as someone who constantly is "stirring things up." Yet, neighborhoods may be characterized not simply by the satisfaction of its activist members and the number and interaction among these leadership strata but also by the duration of activism. Some individuals may be long-term, "seasoned" veterans of the neighborhood; still others may be novices who enter the fray for a single battle and then melt back into the "rank and file."

Our memories of the neighborhoods are clear, and the first impressions significant.... But there is an important lesson for the novice interested in neighborhood observation or citizen action.... One must go beyond windshield survey and the casual walking tour.

D. I. and R. B. Warren
Psychology Today (June 1975): 77–78

The team worker must be alert to the organizational significance of "rooming houses" as well as churches, bars, as well as social agencies, and gang leaders, as well as community "leaders". Keen observation of the neighborhood and its habits, what it considers good and its taboos, is the first requirement of a successful grass-roots organizer.

Martin Oppenheimer and
George Lakey
A Manual for Direct Action,
(Chicago; Quadrangle Books, 1964), p. 28

8 | How to Diagnose a Neighborhood

To all human service organizations, public and private (with or without outreach programs), to school systems and parent-school organizations, civic groups, volunteer agencies and associations, to labor unions and social action groups as well as others who by tradition have treated neighborhoods with a certain sameness, this chapter is for you. Neighborhoods are different. Effective action requires approaches based on subtle but important differences. This chapter describes, step-by-step, a method to capture the distinctive interwoven helping patterns—the networks criss-crossing the neighborhood fabric. Identifying the sources of this uniqueness is the first step in designing effective outreach programs and organizing for citizen action.

The neighborhood ethnography used here was developed to allow trained laypersons to tap into existing networks of helping within a short time period. Thus we not only gather perceptions of key people and events, but we encourage dialogue between residents where we can observe helping and trace down those helped by and those excluded from neighborhood networks. How can some find aid and solace in the neighborhood, while others seek only professional help and still others remain totally isolated in their problem coping? This chapter details the "ethnographic" approach found most effective in seeking answers to these questions.

As we use the term, "neighborhood ethnography" is a comparative research technique based on face-to-face interaction and social-network analysis within and outside of the neighborhood setting. Basic components of the technique include a physical and social mapping, encouraging group dialogue, and sampling different behavior settings in the neighborhood from street corners to back fences to the local supermarket. It is to be noted that the use of this method tends to increase the probability that a local neighborhood will be diagnosed as having a richer and more complex social life than is the case when formal survey sampling techniques are employed.[1]

A. WHICH METHODS ARE BEST? SURVEYS? KEY INFORMANTS? OBSERVATION?

In this chapter we are going to talk in some detail about gathering data on a local neighborhood or community. The first part of our discussion compares several different techniques. If a systematic and extensive statistical picture of a local area is called for, some form of sample survey is generally the best approach. Yet this is usually too expensive or time consuming to design and implement. Peoples' ways of doing things and what they think about their community or their own concerns can be approached using other methods.

These are research techniques that have an applied direction. If you need to justify a program, give "legitimacy" to an approach or idea you already are committed to, collecting survey or observational data may still be a very valuable strategic move: It can help various outside elites be persuaded on the strength of your case.

Perhaps you have just started to think about the problems or needs of a local area. A survey can focus and clarify issues and show priorities. Or it is possible you have an organization that has shown falling attendance at meetings or seems out of touch. Systematic data gathering in the neighborhood may pinpoint weaknesses or failures in the agenda or approach of the organization. These are but a few of the reasons that the neighborhood organizer may wish to borrow, modify, or hire out the talent needed to carry out research in the field.

We will proceed to discuss several methods. Select what you need or skip over what is beyond the scope or style you seek. But even if it is a very descriptive first step, the techniques we will review are tools that can be used to make the assessment which in turn provides the direction of organizer-activist work.

The growth of social-science analysis of problems has largely depended on the use of standardized survey-research techniques. The strength of these approaches also is the source of their greatest weakness: They amass a wealth of complex individual data that is difficult to digest.

Increasingly, the sophistication of probability survey sampling and the elaborate technology required has obscured the role of other methodologies. Unfortunately, when discussions of alternative data-gathering approaches are broached, one is forced into a defensive posture—slogans replace examination of the facts. The cry of "qualitative versus quantitative," "case study versus system analysis," "in-depth versus snapshot," and other dichotomies serve as battle cries on the methodological field of honor.[2]

Seldom are the combined strategies of "atomistic" and "holistic" perspectives utilized. Large numbers of individual interviews—whether highly structured or very exploratory— may be a wasteful investment without careful sampling procedures. At the same time, a few carefully chosen "key informant" interviews can provide much insight into the lives of people in a neighborhood. Whatever technique is used can be greatly aided by a comparative approach—stepping outside of the one setting and going into another adjacent one.

Getting too deeply immersed in the patterns of a single neighborhood—regardless of the specific form of information gathering—will limit the use you can make of the data you obtain. It is important also to identify the type of information you seek. If it is an estimate of the rate of some event—crime, illness, lack of garbage collection, or whatever—then such "behavior reports" must be separated from various values and perceptions which help you to understand the "culture" of a neighborhood. Asking people to give their opinions may provide you with great insight about how events are perceived—and that is important—but it may be a very distorted view of the "quantitative reality." Both are valuable; each is part of a neighborhood diagnosis.

Is there a way out of the dilemma? While not a complete answer, we suggest a direction that may avoid some of the conventional hang-ups. To see this approach in its full sense, it is necessary first to indicate the virtue and the vice of survey sampling on the one hand and traditional ethnography on the other.

When is survey at its best? When the problems it deals with are related to those felt and defined by a given population. In other words, survey is a very good way to take a pulse, to tap a topical problem, to capture a mood of the moment, set it in a frame, and then dissect it.

When is ethnography at its best?[3] When it can capture the unspoken rules, subtle norms that influence people who see the world as a natural outgrowth of their own experiences.

A survey is least useful when the questions asked are the answers to hypotheses and concepts of the researcher and not the sample population. We're not talking here about the conventional issues of reliability and validity but about the intensity and meaning—the importance if you wish—of the questions that the researcher asks as seen by the respondent. As difficult as the problem of refusal and hostility of respondents is for the social researcher, his greatest enemy is really the socially sanctioned acquiescence of the subject—the compliant respondent.

Ethnographic work is least useful and most irresponsible when it disclaims any relation to theory and systematic social process. The curse of the case study is to treat continual observation as an end in itself. This is analogous to the astronomer feeling the immensity of the universe and therefore deciding only to study a few bright stars.

In Chart 10, we have summarized the relative value of using a given data-gathering approach for each of the neighborhood types. The signs shown for each method/ neighborhood combination are the most "efficient" to elicit valid and reliable data. Such ratings depend on the permanence of a designation due to the effects of sampling where population turnover is high or low; the norms of resistance to

Chart 10
Community Structures in Relation
to Data-Gathering Strategies*

	Key Informant	Survey Sampling	Ethnographic
Integral	+	+	+
Parochial	+ −	+ −	+
Diffuse	−	+	+ −
Stepping-stone	+ −	+ −	+
Transitory	−	−	+ −
Anomic	−	+ −	+ −

*Plus and minus signs by each combination refer to the "efficiency" or "power" of a given method—in terms of assessing social structure in a valid and reliable manner. A plus/minus combination means a given method is average in efficiency for a given neighborhood.

outside "intruders" as well as the institutionalized ways to subvert such information gathering; the social distance between neighbors and the researcher; and other factors which are institutional attributes of the neighborhood as a social structure. The ratings in Chart 10 are not based on the "cost" of gathering data per se. Thus where more than one "+" occurs, a given neighborhood setting may be evaluated equally by two methods having equal "power" but different efficiencies. Economic cost is therefore determined in a cost-benefit equation based on personal training and time effort related to the likely valid outcome of their work.

Chart 10 shows several differentials by neighborhood type which reflect (1) whether a given field procedure has an optimal role in a given setting; and (2) what "value added" pattern occurs when more than one method is employed in investigating a specific type of local community. Thus we note that for the integral neighborhood ethnographic methods are very effective; but all three methods show generally high values. In the case of the parochial neighborhood, ethnographic work is highly effective, but survey analysis is not quite as effective as it is in the integral setting. By contrast, for the diffuse neighborhood, survey aggregation is the best single method to employ. For the transitory neighborhood, only the ethnographic approach seems to offer important benefits with little added value attributable to survey and key-informant data gathering.

Finally, in the case of the anomic setting, none of the three methods has great merit. Here the validation of the type is largely a result of finding low levels of social participation, although we cannot be sure whether such data indicates that individuals in such a setting are highly involved in neighborhood social networks or that the measures used merely are inadequate to probe the more discrete levels of clique, family, and intraneighborhood primary group systems which may operate. It is in these senses that the validation of the anomic neighborhood is not enhanced by the use of multiple-investigative techniques. To this degree the anomic neighborhood is a residual category whose character as a "neighborhood" is one lacking social organization in terms of the dimensions of the typology.

Advantages for Cost and Effort

If economic considerations forced us to consider dropping one or more of the data-collection procedures in a particular neighborhood, which might be dropped with the lowest decrease in effectiveness? Returning to the table of ranks and looking at integral areas, we saw it should be aggregated survey. The same holds for parochial, stepping-stone, and transitory neighborhoods. On the other hand, in diffuse and anomic areas we realized that either community ethnography or informant interviewing could be dropped if budgetary limitations so necessitated.

Still another insight gained from the ranking of data-collection procedures by area could be the sequencing of these methods during the data-collection phase of the research. Specifically, if one chooses to conduct the *most efficient* procedure first, then in integral areas the time order of our methods should be informant interviewing, community ethnography, and, finally, aggregated survey. In stepping-stone areas the sequencing would be the same. In both diffuse and anomic neighborhoods we might first conduct surveys then utilize either of the remaining methods. Similar readings of the table of ranks would allow us to predict the time order by efficiency of procedures for the remaining areas.

Our approach assumes that survey data must be evaluated within a framework of social process that is discerned by looking beyond a single observation. It implies a comparative understanding of two critical phenomena: *firstly*, the private character of much of social life, and *secondly*, the necessity for interactive feedback. Both of these principles are violated by survey research, even though they can be somewhat artificially reinstated in the interview situation.

Practitioner ethnography follows two other principles: *firstly*, that the "respondent" has the hypotheses and the theory and is the "teacher"—that the subject is the tutor, and the observer is the student; *secondly*, that there is no assumed sequential cause-and-effect logic to social life. By this we simply mean that people experience problems and other happenings and react to them often with no clearly conscious rationale. Therefore, it is necessary for the observer-researcher to be able to move around in the life space of the subject in order to try to experience the world "as the respondent experiences it."

B. THE ETHOS OF NEIGHBORHOOD ETHNOGRAPHY: A PRACTICAL STEP-BY-STEP GUIDE[2]

These remarks are meant to set the stage on the ethnographic side of our study design because so often it is simply assumed that such efforts are wholly exploratory and preliminary in character or simply ways to embellish or give "authenticity" to the cold statistics of survey research.

The methodology employed in this ethnographic work consists of a form of open-ended interview-and-observation effort using a set of guiding concepts and dimensions of local community and can function systematically to assess the neighborhood and community as a behavioral setting for help giving and getting.

The knowledge gained from this type of research has a variety of implications, one of which is for the way that social services should be organized. By investigating how different populations solve problems, we will be able to qualify what constitutes a resource for a given population and to describe the nature of the problem-coping processes surrounding those formal and informal resources. In this way, this kind of study can provide valuable insights that have direct implication for citizens and organizations to be better equipped to plan service interventions that are consistent with the unique coping styles, culture, and helping networks of a given population.

Gaining Entrée:
City Hall Has Its Place

When you first arrive in a community, it's a good idea to spend a short time getting a feel for the city as a whole. Go to city hall and look around—note the location of the building. Is it near other community service centers such as the library, the courthouse, a general community center, the social service offices? Where is the central business district? What else is available within the immediate vicinity? What offices are housed in the building itself? Who are the city officers? What type of government does the city have—city council? mayoral? City Manager? Usually the names of these persons are readily available—you won't have to make an appointment with any official to get this information. Use your eyes and your head; there's got to be a building directory, and there are usually pamphlets telling about the city and city services on display. Pick them up and look them over. This type of general background information will give you a hint as to what's available from the city and how accessible these services are. Background that will help you in understanding what the people in the neighborhoods might be talking about or concerned with.

Maps

Maps are probably the most important and useful items that you will be able to garner from the city hall. They are vital and usually are available at only a minimal cost. Get two *street maps* of the city: one for yourself to make notes on, and one to use in interview situations.

Make sure you get street maps and not precinct maps. The precinct maps have dark lines outlining voting districts and may be confusing in cases where voting precincts do not correspond with elementary school districts or what people in general think of as "their" neighborhood.

Find the sample neighborhoods on the map. On "your" map only, outline the neighborhoods. You can pinpoint services, business districts, etc. A good map enables you quickly and clearly to see "your" neighborhood in relation to other neighborhoods and to the city in general; it enables you to locate people all over the community.

The Phone Book

The telephone book for your area is usually available free from the telephone company. All you have to do is to request it and give a phone number—either your own home phone or where you work. The phone book is a great time-saver. Carry it with you for easy access to addresses and numbers. Use it at home to set up appointments, to contact referrals, and to find churches and pastors. Or just thumb through it to familiarize yourself with the area.

The Library

It's a good idea to drop by the library while you're on your initial data-gathering mission. The usefulness of the information available there, in respect to the neighborhoods themselves, varies from city to city, but usually available are listings on adult-education offerings, city recreation programs, and senior-citizen's activities that will help to build your background regarding the community at large. Some communities have neighborhood-focused programs stemming from the library such as bookmobiles or children's films in neighborhood parks. It's good to know about these in advance.

Newspapers

Pick up a copy of the local newspaper. This will brief you on current community issues and events. Be sure to check the "Community Calendar" for events that might be occurring in the neighborhood—potluck suppers, block parties, etc. A glance at the want ads can tell you about garage or yard sales and also can give you some idea about the selling prices of homes in the various areas of the city.

The Chamber of Commerce

The chamber of commerce should have a list of community organizations and contact persons that is available at a small cost—usually from $0.50–$2.50. This list is an invaluable source of potential neighborhood contacts. Go over the list and locate the presidents of various organizations on your map. Find out where they live. If any of these people live in "your" neighborhood, you're in luck. Through their public listing, you can feel free to call them and ask for an appointment to talk with them about their neighborhood. Usually the organizations represented on the Chamber of Commerce list run the gambit from the PTA to M.O.M.S. (Mothers of Men in Service), from the local bicycle club to the lapidary society.

It usually will not be necessary to explain yourself or your mission to any of the above institutions in order to get the information you seek. If you do happen across an inquisitive bureaucrat, tell the truth about why you are there. You do not have to adopt any role in order to legitimate or justify yourself. These are the places that people turn to for information, and your requests are in no way suspect or unusual.

Once you have received the basic information you need from these city-wide institutions, *STOP!!* If, in the course of your work in the neighborhoods, you are referred to certain city-wide agencies or officials, you can always go back to talk with them; but the focus of study is the neighborhood, and you should have enough background information by now to proceed.

C. TAPPING INTO THE NETWORKS

Familiarizing Yourself with the Area

Drive through the area. Map businesses, parks, schools, and any other important or interesting landmarks. Get a feel for housing type, activity level, and the geographical make-up of the neighborhood. Record your impressions, either in notes or on tape if a recorder is available. Then, park the car and survey on foot.

Even though you can cover more territory faster by driving, you are not making the most effective use of your survey time. It isn't necessary to map every house on every street; just get a feel for the area and the people. Maximize use of interaction—stop and chat with people who are out, and *keep your eyes open*. It isn't necessary to carry a pad and pencil or even a map if you've familiarized yourself with the streets. Just remember where you've been and make note of it later. Record your initial impressions as fully as possible—you can go back to them after working in the area for a while and check for clues to dimensions that might not have been brought out in your talks with informants. If your initial impressions and the information you've received don't jell, this can point out pathways that you should pursue. For instance: if you noted a poorer or sloppier area of the neighborhood, but no one you are referred to lives there, find out why. Or if you noticed some physical characteristic of the homes, such as porch chairs, but you've never seen anyone sitting in them, maybe you should try going into the neighborhood at a different time—in the evening or on the weekend—to see if the chairs really are indicative of interneighbor interaction.

Defining the Boundaries

A neighborhood can be many things to many people. Since elementary school districts represent jurisdictional definitions, and since the "real" neighborhood boundaries and school-district boundaries may not correspond, in the course of your field experience you may find it necessary to redefine the neighborhood. If so, proceed by lopping off sections of the area rather than by dividing the area into subneighborhoods and then rating them separately. Here are some conditions under which you might wish to eliminate a part of the area.

1. Major Physical Boundaries. Highways, rivers, major streets that cut through the area and isolate some section from the core of the neighborhood.
2. Historical Affiliation. If an area of the elementary school district has only recently been annexed, and there is evidence that this area is not really a part of the neighborhood, or if it maintains allegiance with its former area.
3. City Boundaries. Some school districts exceed the city borders and draw students from neighboring communities. Unless there is evidence for including the other community as a part of the neighborhood, stick to the community under study.

We recognize that many neighborhoods house two or more social classes or ethnic groups. This, of itself, is not enough evidence to divide the neighborhood into its subareas. We are interested in observing the interaction between the areas and in discovering the nature and intensity of social similarities and differences that may exist. Arguments for subdivision must be based on observed interaction, values, and norms—not on housing characteristics, social class, or ethnic affiliation alone.

Making Use of What's There

Here are some ideas of things to be on the lookout for while in the neighborhood.

1. Houses for Sale. Where are they? Are they clustered or dispersed throughout the area? Are any for sale by the owner? If so, go and look at it. What realtors are handling the sale of homes? Are these realtors locally based?
2. Construction and Home Repair. Note any homes being fixed up. Who's doing the work—neighbors or a construction company? What time of the day is the work being done?
3. Coffee Shops, Restaurants, and Bars. Are they locally oriented or franchise? Who frequents them?
4. Service Institutions. Are there any in the neighborhood? What type of services do they offer? Are they focused toward the neighborhood or the greater area?
5. Clubs and Organizations. Are there any clubhouses here? Or hints that local organizations exist, such as a street sign urging you to drive carefully installed by the Pleasant Pines Homeowner's Association?
6. Churches. What denominations are represented? Who is the pastor? Does he/she live in the area? (Check in your phone book.)
7. Stores. Do they service local customers, or are they areal in orientation? What type of merchandise is available in the area?
8. Parks. Are they well maintained? Who frequents the parks? What facilities are available? How many people are there?
9. Garage and Yard Sales. Stop in. Who's running the sale? Is one family selling goods on behalf of several neighbors? Are groups in the neighborhood participat-

ing? Notice what type of merchandise is on sale. Look at brand names, prices. Start up conversations if possible. It is not necessary to push for information—take your cues from what is for sale.

10. Type and Make of Vehicles. Are they old or new, large or small? Is there on street parking? Are there recreational vehicles, foreign cars, station wagons, trucks.

11. Window Signs and Bumper Stickers. Are there any signs or stickers on display? What do they say? Is there a topical concentration, or are thematic signs fairly well dispersed?

12. General Appearance and Upkeep. Is it uniform throughout the area? Are there fences, pools, swing sets?

13. Activity level. Take note of the time of day, the time of year, and (in more changeable climes) weather conditions. Look for evidence of activity if no one's about. You can check your impressions later by talking with people

14. People's Reactions to You. Do they stare? Wave? Smile? Do they look out furtively from behind the blinds or offer "nice day" as they walk by?

15. Social Interaction. Is it hostile or friendly? Are people going from house to house, talking over fences, etc.?

You should not spend more than two or two-and-a-half hours on the initial survey. Observe and take note of what's available in the area. You will always have slack time when you're in the field for further investigation—and a better idea of how to spend your time after more contact with the area residents themselves.

If no one's out in the neighborhood, don't despair. You haven't wasted your time. You know the streets, the houses, the layout, and you should have some clues as to what the people do. Now is the time to go to your lists, to set up appointments, and to make contact with the people who live in the neighborhood.

Making Contact

In your initial survey you may have happened onto people— on the street, at garage sales, etc.—who have been willing to talk with you about their neighborhood. Most likely you didn't, or when you tried to press for the type of information needed, you were met with silence. Don't worry. It is not likely that most people will open up to strangers in a public setting. What you have learned from them is very valuable and a test against what people will tell you in a more formal situation.

Now, however, is the time to get into longer, deeper conversations with neighborhood residents. Whom do you go to? Hopefully, your list of organizational chairpersons from the chamber of commerce has someone from the neighborhood. If so, this is a good place to start. Especially if the person is not heavily tied in with the neighborhood institutions, i.e., PTA, church, school, etc. Call them and ask for an appointment. You must be ready to answer questions about your presence and purpose in the neighborhood. People on the list will probably be willing to talk to you and will supply you with valuable background information for approaching the more formal channels. Your contact probably will give you referrals to other of her/his friends and neighbors.

The Elementary-School Principal

Your best bet is to get to the elementary-school principal pretty soon. Call and make an appointment; it might be necessary to get the approval of the school superintendent before the principal is allowed to talk with you. The principal has a wealth of information about the neighborhood and is especially informative in fields that you might have difficulty probing in home situations. He/she can give you a general overview of the neighborhood; home values, occupational makeup, percentage of single-parent families, demographic similarities or differences, estimated income levels, and leisure-time activities of the residents. The principal should be aware of any particular church influence, especially if a number of the children attending the school go to any one church. In addition, the principal is a valuable source regarding the incidence of A.D.C. and welfare support, and the frequency and type of child abuse in the neighborhood.

It is important to determine the nature and the depth of the principal's involvement in the neighborhood in order to do a comparative analysis of the effectiveness of principals in inducing or sustaining neighborhood cohesion.

Finally, the principal can give you easy referral access to some important people in the neighborhood. You should find out the names of neighborhood leaders and activists such as the PTA president or the head of the volunteer program (if the school has one). Ask the principal to identify the "chronic griper" and any persons who are active with groups like boy scouts, little league, etc., that are important to the area. Give the principal the chance to initiate other references, and remember to let her/him talk—you can gain valuable information by letting the principal carry the conversational ball.

Don't Forget These Folks

Here is a list of people to be on the watch for in "your" neighborhood. All of these may not be represented in any one area. These are suggestions of the type of people you should ask about and possibilities for contacting if you feel you need further information or are not satisfied with the quality of the information you are receiving.

1. Elementary School Principal. This is a MUST.
2. Pastors. Talk to the pastor of any church located in the neighborhood if he/she is also a neighborhood resident. If you discover that a large segment of the neighborhood population attends a specific church, make an effort to see the clergyman regardless of where he lives. You may find that church affiliation is not a crucial factor in the neighborhood. In that case, don't spend too much time in church-affiliated channels.
3. PTA Presidents and School Volunteer Organizers. Another must. Try to assess the effectiveness and involvement of the PTA. If there is a volunteer organization, in what ways does it differ from the PTA? Do the memberships overlap? These contacts can be asked to set up group meetings or to invite their friends over to talk with you.

4. Chronic Griper. Ask people you meet with to identify the "chronic griper" of the neighborhood. If there is one, be sure to contact her/him. This person's information usually differs in telling ways from the overall picture presented by the more usual resident.

5. Presidents of Clubs and Social Organizations. If any of these people live in your neighborhood, it's good to meet with them. Find out if the club is neighborhood based. Referrals gained from these contacts are good checks against the more formal referral networks. If the president of a city-wide organization, like the League of Women Voters, lives in the neighborhood, he/she is also a good source of information about other neighborhoods in the community.

6. Homeowner's Associations. If you discover a homeowner's association that is presently, or once has been, active in the area, make an effort to talk with someone involved with that association. Even if the association is now defunct, you want to know what it did do and why it has disbanded.

7. Boy Scouts, Girl Scouts, Little League. If organizations like these are active, talk with their leaders. This is one way of making contact with men in the neighborhood.

8. Neighborhood and Community Leaders. If anyone is identified as a leader, talk with her/him. Find out what leaders do and why certain people are considered to be leaders.

9. Realtors. Realtors can give you good demographic information about the city and the neighborhood— population groups, income brackets, etc.—and they can set this information in an historical perspective.

10. Local Business People. These people can be good contacts, especially if the business services the neighborhood primarily. Examples: "Ma & Pa store," a local bar, etc.

11. Service Agencies. If there are any service agencies in the neighborhood, drop in. Caution: most service agencies have a broad, area-wide clientele and may not be particularly useful in neighborhood studies.

12. The "Deviant." Try to isolate the types of "deviants" in

the neighborhood: social, property, sexual. You may want to make an effort to talk with one, especially if you sense that your regular contacts are feeding you a line.

13. People with Special Economic Roles. If you find out about anyone in the neighborhood who has a special economic role—anything from babysitting in the home to a home-based construction company—contact that person. Policemen, firemen, and their ilk are especially good sources of this type of information.

14. Referrals. Be sure to follow along at least two separate referral pathways. It is important to see if the networks overlap or if they present different pictures of the neighborhood. Entrance to referral pathways should be generated from independent initial contacts, and these contacts should be as socially diverse as possible. E.g., the elementary-school principal, and the president of the bowling league.

15. Age Groups. Try to meet with someone from different age groups. If there are a lot of senior citizens in "your" neighborhood, make an effort to contact them. If there are a lot of teenagers, go over to a group and start a conversation.

16. Ethnic Groups. Be sure to make contact with members of all relevant ethnic groups. This may be a significant source of helping/referral and may link this neighborhood to community-wide networks.

A Note on "The Key Informant"

It is advisable to set up interviews with certain "key informants"—persons who you believe will have a knowledge of the total community, a sense of history. Principals are an example of this type of individual. When you believe someone holds a potential wealth of general and important information, go in a twosome. One can write while one directs the discussion, and immediate debriefing to get down the many fine points will allow you both to profit from the neighborhood perspective.

Remember, it is not necessary for you to talk with someone on every block or at every other house. Your job is to identify networks, pursue them, and to discover how the neighborhood operates.

Chit-Chat

During the first few minutes of your visit, both you and your host are likely to feel strained and uncomfortable. Chit-chat helps to break down this tension and to set the tone for a free-flowing conversation. You can talk about anything—the weather, something in the house, the traffic—make small talk and establish trust.

Explain Your Presence

Give a quick run-down of your interest. Mention that you're trying to find out what holds a neighborhood together and how people help each other in this neighborhood. Ask for questions. Answer any questions truthfully. Some people will require a fuller knowledge of the scope of your presence than others. Be willing and able to satisfy them with all the information that they want. Use your discretion here—it isn't necessary to bore the host with a twenty-minute detailed description of your theoretical perspective, but it is necessary to eliminate any doubts that the neighborhood residents may have about you, your legitimacy, or your motives.

Neighborhood Definition

We have defined a neighborhood as an elementary-school district for several reasons, among which are that it is a compromise unit with an institutional focus, and that it provides a manageable area for observation within a limited time span. But it is important to find out how the residents define their neighborhood. Some people see their neighborhood as "just this block," others as the whole city. Bring out your unmarked map and ask the informant to tell you what he/she thinks of as his/her neighborhood. People will usually start talking about their immediate neighborhood and then their extended connections throughout the area. Listen, and encourage the informant to continue. Get information about churches, shopping areas, housing, gathering places—anything physical. Ask if the neighborhood has a name, and how the informant tells other people in the city where he/she lives. Find out about residential mobility, houses for sale. The resident of the neighborhood knows more about this than you do, and may well get carried away with his/her own expertise and give you information you wouldn't have been able to know about or to discover through directed questioning.

Follow Up Leads

During her/his description of the neighborhood, the informant has probably mentioned points or issues that pertain directly to your objectives. Follow up on these leads now. The informant may have mentioned areas where the residents hold block parties, streets where friends live, or homes that are sloppy. Find out more about the leads they have given you, and *do* direct the conversation toward helping networks or activities. But, base your questions on the foundations that the informant has already established.

Initiate New Subjects

By now you've probably established a basis of trust with the informant. He/she may have asked what else you want to know. Remember the objectives of your visit and hit upon points that have not been covered yet. Two methods of inquiry are useful when the informant does not really seem to understand what you want.

Draw upon your own experience. You've lived in at least one neighborhood in your life, and you've had contact with many, many people and situations in your work in other neighborhoods. Draw examples from your own experience to illustrate situations you are concerned with—what people do at the time of death; how men help each other with construction or home repair; the activities of volunteer groups at school or church. This type of exchange of information is important. You can't expect people to open up to you if you just sit there silently recording their every word. By opening up yourself, you reassure the informant, and make it easier for her/him to talk with you.

Propose a hypothetical situation. There are some topics that are taboo for certain people. Remember the gentlemanly edict that politics and religion are not topics for polite discussion. When you feel you are treading near the boundaries of a forbidden or sensitive subject, or one that is threatening to the people you are talking with, don't push it through direct questioning. Proposing a hypothetical situation is a good way to get information regarding commitment to the neighborhood, child abuse, treatment of deviants, etc.

Hypothetical situations are "What if?" questions: What if you won the lottery? Would you move? What if someone moved into the neighborhood who abused her/his children? What if you needed your house rewired? What if someone is causing trouble? Frequently the informants will respond to your hypothetical formulation with concrete examples of what *does* happen in their neighborhood.

Get Referrals

Ask about leaders, friends—people you should talk with, or people whom the informant knows whom he/she thinks would be willing to talk with you.

Let the Informant Close the Interview

When you feel that you have covered all the points you are concerned with, don't just pack up and go. Ask if there's anything more the informant thinks is important of interest about her/his neighborhood. You may have missed something very important and, at least, this gives the informant a time to express her/his own gripes or concerns.

D. THE MORE THE MERRIER: SOME HELPFUL FIELD IDEAS

There are certain situations when you will want to have two ethnographers working together at one meeting with informants—in group discussions and key-informant interviews.

The Group Discussion

Group discussions are fantastic ways to cover a lot of territory quickly. If at all possible, you should try to set up at least one such situation in each neighborhood. You can ask neighborhood organizational people, e.g., PTA, to get some of their members together to talk with you; or you can suggest that a contact invite some friends and neighbors over for your visit. You've got a room full of people, all hooked into the same network—a ready-made lab situation for observing interaction. Note who's there and who isn't. Find out where the people live.

Group situations almost always flow more freely than the one-on-one interview. You need two ethnographers just to record the information. One person's tale elicits another's, and the situation may approach mayhem. In order to gain the most from the group discussion, the members of the ethnographic team must be attuned with one another. Their pacing is vital—one can write while the other talks, or, they may find themselves each involved in separate conversation groups. The team should reconstruct the discussion *immediately* afterward in order not to lose the sense of what happened and in order to record anecdotes that the ethnographers were not able to take full notes on. An hour's debriefing is usually the minimum time allotted here to record all the many anecdotes as accurately as possible.

Slack Time: Time Well Spent

There's always going to be a lot of time between interviews, or at lunch and dinner time, when you won't be scheduled to meet with anyone. Spend as much of this time in the neighborhood as possible. If there are restaurants or bars in the area, eat there. Go to the stores, parks, or hangouts. Cover garage and yard sales. Look at homes for sale. These informal contacts are more meaningful once you have some concrete knowledge of the neighborhood. You can always work on your field notes in the local coffee shop—if someone asks you what you're doing, tell them. It's a good conversation opener.

Getting into the Home

You may be invited in by someone you meet on the street, but don't count on it. The best entree is to get appointments— from lists, from previous contacts, or from general information about the neighborhood. Call beforehand and allow yourself enough time to let the conversation flow.

Take note of the physical properties of the home, exterior and interior. Any special aspects, such as a lovely garden, handmade objects, paintings, or construction work, are good conversation openers. You should pay attention to the furnishings, upkeep, and general style of the home.

The Sustained Ethnographic Interview

Remember—as an ethnographer, you are *not* a formal interviewer. There are certain items you do want to get at, but this information should evolve out of the informant's framework, not yours. Take your time and find things out indirectly. Follow their leads, don't cut them off, LISTEN—the informant will undoubtedly mention topics that you're concerned with. Follow up on these points before delving into unintroduced areas.

Before you go out for an interview, familiarize yourself thoroughly with the organizer's exercises at the conclusion of each chapter. Make notes of the information you want to get. One or two words should do. These notes are to remind you of points that you want to cover. They are *not* to be an interview format or a list of specific questions to ask. You can glance at this list during the course of your visit to see what further information you need to get. Go over these notes quickly if the phone rings or if your host is out of the room, then try to guide the conversation toward the uncovered areas.

As you gain experience, you will probably find some means of structuring the conversation that you feel comfortable with. This should grow from your experience in the field situation, not from intellectual theorizing as to the "proper" logical order of an interview.

Open Time—Contingency Plans

Leave time open after talking with persons who might be key informants, the elementary-school principal, etc. These people might call while you are present to set up meetings for you right away with neighbors—and you should be flexible. Have in mind a contingency plan in case this doesn't happen—you could go up to the messiest house in the neighborhood and ask the owners if they'd talk with you or interview the local shopkeepers.

Travel Time

The time you spend driving to and from the community can be some of your most productive hours. Rehash your day; talk it out. Fill in notes and embellish stories. A lot of the information you've received is intuitive. It is important to verbalize your impressions in order to crystallize what you *do* know. Work up hypotheses about neighborhood interaction and formalize plans for testing them. You can plan your future work in the neighborhood—who you should see, what you need to look for, and how to go about it. Debrief and discuss.

Budgeting Time

It should not take more than four-and-a-half field hours to complete the initial community data gathering and the neighborhood survey. You may not feel that you have all the information you need, but there's sure to be slack time during the days you've scheduled interviews, and this can be most effectively used in walking about the neighborhood, shopping, or just hanging out.

Scheduling Interviews

After you have a bit of a feel for the area, it's time to schedule interviews. Set up interviews in advance. Allow a minimum of two to two-and-a-half hours between the beginnings of interviews. You can spend the slack time in informal neighborhood interaction. Try to fill your field days as full as possible. You should be in the neighborhood during all times of day. Evenings are good for meeting the men or with women employed outside the home or for talking with families. A morning interview, two in the afternoon, and one in the evening is not unreasonable.

Monitoring Yourself

You should be aware of yourself and your effect on the residents in all field experiences. Dress appropriately for the neighborhood and the situation—don't alienate someone by your dress or demeanor before you get a chance to talk with her/him. Pay attention to what you do and to the type of responses your actions elicit. Make note of this. Watch for body cues—note seating arrangements and their effects on interviews. In your interactions with the neighborhood residents, you cannot be the isolated observer. The residents are making as many judgments about you as you are about them. Act accordingly.

Keeping a Record

It is necessary to record both your observations and your impressions daily. Anthropologists have a tradition of keeping a field journal on "empirical" observations and a field diary of their personal impressions and reactions. This is a good policy for neighborhood ethnographers to follow. As you gain knowledge of an area, you can go back and check your impressions, change your judgments if necessary, and uncover pathways of investigation that you should follow.

Take as complete a set of notes as possible. It will be easier to take notes in some interview situations than in others. Try to be complete, but remember that eye contact is important in maintaining conversation flow. Record as many direct quotes and stories as possible—these are invaluable. They hold a sense of the people, of the neighborhood, that retelling cannot match.

Steering an Honest Course

In neighborhood ethnography, it is at times tempting to assume a role, to tell a story, in order to legitimize or justify yourself in the neighborhood. In all cases we must caution against such deception. Although you may gain immediate access, entree, or information by disguising your real purpose in the neighborhood, role-playing can backfire, and whatever you may have gained in the short run can result in a long-term loss of legitimacy.

Neighborhoods are not very big, and news travels fast. When you don't know the networks that exist in the area, you risk losing all access by being caught in a pose. Don't back yourself into a corner.

The "Dynamic-duo" Approach to Neighborhood Ethnography

Experience suggests that the optimal ethnographic approach is to pair two people in one community. This is possible where randomization of elementary-school districts has allowed for work in two neighborhoods within reasonably close proximity to each other.

While each person is responsible for the main organizing,

interviewing, mapping, and analysis of her/his neighborhood, there are many advantages to using the "dynamic-duo" approach. First, going in as a team allows you to check out your impressions and to compare notes. This may be done while driving, over lunch at the local "Burger Queen" (or exotic little bistro), or at any other times when your paths might cross.

Second, your teammate may be drawn upon as a resource person. There are two basic plusses to this. For one thing, whenever you are facing a situation where you feel it is best to have two ethnographers in on the action, this is the person to whom you have immediate access. This is a matter of scheduling in advance so that both of you will be available to chat with groups, certain key informants, and school principals in *both* neighborhoods.

As an outgrowth of this team interview, you will have made certain observations that would have been denied you had you been confined to one neighborhood. For example, while driving to an interview in your teammate's neighborhood you will take note of the differences in housing characteristics, interaction patterns, status display, etc. You may note certain things that have not as yet been noted by your teammate. Such observations should be shared as they may encourage your teammate to explore different pathways. During the interview itself, you may hear issues raised that were not as yet mentioned by residents of "your" neighborhood. You may then want to bring these up as "having heard about some other issues when you were talking with residents from another part of the city," when you are back in "your" neighborhood. The corollary to this is that you may (with your teammate's prior consent) bring up issues that are salient to "your" respondents but which, as yet, have been unexplored in your teammate's neighborhood.

When you are asked at some later point in time to compare your neighborhood with others in the community, you will then have a somewhat better perspective than that gleaned from your work in only one neighborhood.

A Final Word

Let the following advise serve as a postscript to what we have already indicated. By all means make note of the effect you think your presence might have on future neighborhood interactions. Remember, you are there to look at behaviors, examine values, and discover support networks in the neighborhood. But you should be aware that the presence of outsiders always represents a potential source of change, however minimal and however unintentional. Please note your impressions and put them in writing.

Organizer's Exercises
Chapter 8

PHYSICAL DESCRIPTION OF THE NEIGHBORHOOD

1. Includes a mapping of each block in terms of housing characteristics (single dwelling, age, size, and construction). Description should also note areas of commercial development, churches, meeting places, and important natural barriers suggesting internal differentiation of the total area.

2. Special physical attributes include evidence of political activity (signs, stickers, etc.)

3. Types of automobiles and special decorative features of homes (e.g., lampposts, grillwork, painting of homes).

4. Evidence of general upkeep and neighborhood improvements or lack of service:

    Neighborhood appearance and upkeep:

0	1	2	3	4	5	6	7	8	9
Poor									Excellent

5. What is the extent to which the neighborhood has a physically isolated boundary? (You should indicate on each boundary how many are marked by major subdivisions, by differences in housing, by physical barriers, or in contrast where there is little differentiation between the end of this neighborhood and the beginning of another. Therefore, the discussion should include each of the directions and what is true of them.)

Physical isolation of area from the rest of city in terms of its boundaries:

0	1	2	3	4	5	6	7	8	9
Physically								Physically	
Separated								blends in	

6. What are the number and variety of behavior settings that are found in the neighborhood? (Here we are speaking about parks and recreation areas, local stores or churches, street corners, back fences, any special settings that can bring people together.)

   a. Number of *potential* gathering places observed in the neighborhood:

0	1	2	3	4	5	6	7	8	9
None									Many

   b. Number of *observed* gathering places:

0	1	2	3	4	5	6	7	8	9
None									Many

   c. Diversity of potential gathering places:

0	1	2	3	4	5	6	7	8	9
None									Much

   d. Diversity of observed gathering places:

0	1	2	3	4	5	6	7	8	9
None									Much

   e. Competition over gathering places:

0	1	2	3	4	5	6	7	8	9
None									Much

7. What is the extent of demographic similarities, i.e., homogeneity versus heterogeneity of the neighborhood? (This includes how similar people are in regard to social characteristics such as age, family life cycle—preschool children versus teenage children—income, education, occupation, ethnic-group identification, etc. It may be possible to point out that a neighborhood has two different, evenly divided groups or several groups or a majority of one group and a minority of another or whatever helps spell out the diversity of the area.)

0	1	2	3	4	5	6	7	8	9
Homogeneous							Heterogeneous		

If there are remoter nations that wish us not good but ill, they know that we are strong; they know we can and will defend our neighborhoods.

Franklin D. Roosevelt
Quoted in Webster's *Third International Dictionary*

Neighborhoods are composed of people who enter by the very fact of birth or chosen residence into a common life.

Lewis Mumford,
The Urban Prospect
New York: (Harcourt Brace & World, 1968), p. 59.

9 | **Neighborhoods and Democracy:** Some Comments on Societal Change

Beyond the family, the neighborhood is the most universal base of social life to be found in any society. It requires no membership and pays no wages, and yet we belong actively or passively to a neighborhood.

Standing midway between the household and the larger society, this universal social group often mirrors the needs and aspirations of the individual on the one hand, and of societal norms and expectations on the other. People do not join neighborhoods. And yet all of us partake of neighborhood life—good, bad, or indifferent. There is a competitive market for the identity, the allegiance, loyalty, and participation of the individual.

Neighborhood as a meaningful social entity is not merely an abstraction or idealized harmony of interests. Rather, in a profoundly practical way it has a valuable role to play in the lives of urban dwellers—whether they be inner city, peripheral, suburban, or exurban.

Who Needs Neighborhoods?

One of the most highly touted ideas of the 1960s was neighborhood social engineering (urban renewal, Model Cities, and various other programs.) Although many of these programs remain with us to this day, most of them were fairly unsuccessful. The purpose of this handbook has been to review what we know today about neighborhoods and apply that to the varying realistic needs of the urban citizen.

In recent years there has been a critical review of the

social intervention potential of local residential neighborhoods. This has accompanied a series of significant experiments in political and administrative decentralization in several large urban areas. As yet no definitive evaluation of these experiments has been produced, nor has any cumulative or generalizable knowledge base on which to develop such an assessment been constructed. There has also been a reaction against overzealous optimism from the late 1960s. This has resulted in a restricted flow of governmental funds into new programs of local control and action in the 1970s. In addition, a research thrust devaluing the role of territoriality in urban community structure has occurred. Academically and administratively, the position of the neighborhood is presently in a state of partial eclipse. But there is evidence of a citizen movement counter to these trends. In this final portion of our "tour" through neighborhoods, some key guideposts direct our discussion:

(1) What are the elements of a sound and viable neighborhood?[1]

(2) For what problems and for which populations is the neighborhood the most salient structure for social participation and social program intervention?

(3) What is the future of the neighborhood as a planning and socially meaningful entity in the urban context?

In fact, all of these concerns are really facets of the same problem of attempting to gauge and control the rise or decline of territorial units within the urbanized areas of American metropolitan centers. Such a basic focus often is translated into the language of "social indicators" and "quality of life" of a local area. These are elusive dimensions whose measurement has become of major concern to federal, state, and local public-service agencies. In humanistic terms it is of growing concern to urban dwellers themselves—whether suburban, inner city, low income, or the relatively affluent.

There is no reason to question the goals of the neighborhood movement in America. But it is important to raise questions about the wisdom of each of us hanging on it so many of our hopes for urban salvation and for the autonomous urban village. To take this approach is to lose perspective on the fact that neighborhood is but one aspect of urban human existence. In focusing solely on the nurturing of neighborhood ties, we may neglect the fact that there is a need to maintain and strengthen many of the other personal relationships based on mutual interest which are not capable of being served by residential proximity.

The traditional way of defining the neighborhood in geographical terms is in need of revision. The city, seen as a mosaic of neighborhoods with relatively small urban areas and intense interaction within their boundaries is basically a romantic fiction. Frequently, we long for such a world in the face of the perceived inroads of the mass society.

But one may well ask: "Are neighborhoods obsolete?" Can we look upon the criss-crossing of expressways through neighborhoods, the urban renewal, urban development, and other sorts of inroads as the disinvestment in older areas which has plagued the reality of urban neighborhood life? Can we see any real hope for the maintenance of viable local areas? Is this context of more diffuse and weaker social ties a basis for meaningful human relationships?

The easy physical access and the social networks which are no longer synonymous with physical proximity certainly must be incorporated in the picture that we have of urban reality. Neighborhoods do play important roles, often as way-stations, often as ways of assimilating the newcomer to urban life. There is a multitude of functions other than that of facilitating intimate social relations. "Nonintimate" bridging social ties are vital resources and may be seen as an essential if not the modal pattern of social reality in urban neighborhoods. As such, they are expressed by the rise of such nontraditional forms as the stepping-stone, transitory, and integral neighborhoods. These may indeed be the prototypical forms for neighborhood vitality in contemporary society, rather than the traditional parochial or homogeneous diffuse types.

Furthermore, territorially defined social units may be more dominant within particular ethnic groups or at a given stage of organization. Historical and cultural patterns, racial, socioeconomic or sexual discrimination—all these factors tend to restrict access to alternative social units. Blacks, women, or families with young children, as well as the retired or low-income family rely more on local neighborhood. Thus, the spatially proximate base of social linkage is likely to vary depending on a number of demographic characteristics of the individual. For there are stages in the life cycle when the multiple values that neighborhood provide do indeed exist. There are the child-bearing years, and there are also the series of local institutions that the senior citizens may rely on for convenience and access.

We can read into these ebbing-and-flowing increases in the function of neighborhood a restoration of some earlier localized lifestyle. Neighborhoods themselves may provide the stimulus for movement into wider social groups. Indeed, there may be ways to create within a small scale the diversity of social values and lifestyles which is a vital part of the nurturing of the democratic spirit.

To serve as a radical or social-class amalgam runs contrary to the often preservative and conservative role that the neighborhood plays. But if we must view the neighborhood as the haven in which individuals protect themselves against the incessant pressures for social change, we much not overlook the fact that the neighborhood with its social networks is often the basis for coping and problem-solving resources that are critical in allowing individuals to adjust to the shocks of the larger society.

In a very fundamental way, this vital source of adaptive capacity expressed by the neighborhood as a local community and the necessarily homogenizing basis of creating such a secure anchor run counter to some of the best ideas of social planners and advocates of perfection of the democratic ethic. Yet this should not be cause for discouragement and pessimism. Examination of the necessary ingredients which permit neighborhoods to function as significant social entities cannot be based on other than the realities of human behavior. If the neighborhood is to serve these functions for individuals, we must recognize the prerequisites as they exist, not as we would wish them to be.

It is not the question of political meanings of neighborhoods to which we address ourselves. The fight for community self-determination should closely identify with the fight for neighborhood self-determination. The question which we began with—"Who needs neighborhoods?"—is best answered by saying that, indeed, all of us do. The useful functions that neighborhoods perform successfully must be encouraged by a public policy which, although it should not legislate the creation of such neighborhoods, can and should foster the emergence of their positive qualities. The neighborhood as a meaningful entity is not so much an ideological goal but one which takes on a profoundly practical meaning in the lives of urban dwellers.

Emphasis on neighborhoods at the expense of other important bases of community can create a danger of new myths which replace the old ones. What is needed is a more valid perspective in which urban neighborhood ties are seen as a crucial linkage in a complex of important human relationships.

A more realistically specific approach is possible. The role of community intervention, which involves the local neighborhood, must be aided by better "mapping" of the urban community. Our schema offers one such approach. The efforts of community change, ranging from the Model Cities program to Saul Alinsky-type "grass-roots" organizing,[2] have simply not had the tools necessary for sophisticated neighborhood analysis. Too often, mere administrative definitions of neighborhoods have been used to define the real parameters of neighborhood social organization. Moreover, the use of convenient uniformities of definition such as "low income," "ghetto," "suburb," "working class," "middle class," and other stereotypes have prevented organizers and policymakers from taking into account meaningful definitions of neighborhood.

Each of these settings can be seen as having some capacity to facilitate, resist, or institute change. In some cases they are

innovative and generate new values and norms and are able
to receive new ideas and influences.

Neighborhoods and Problem-Solving Systems

We have treated neighborhoods in social-structural rather
than ideological terms. Each form has a different potential
with respect to change; each has the capacity to generate
own institutional processes. In the handbook we have been
able to compare the capacity of a variety of neighborhoods,
particularly the capacity to generate problem-coping systems
and problem solutions. Each type of neighborhood tends to
develop a different capacity in that regard.

One of the most basic issues addressed here in the *Handbook* is this: Under what conditions is the local neighborhood a
cost-effective point of social intervention? When does the investment in outreach efforts aimed at neighborhood versus
the work place, family, or the individual per se provide the
optimum payoff? If an agency or citizen group wants to be
effective, is the neighborhood a preferred base of operations?
In some instances (the anomic area) the answer—given limited resources and staff—is going to be "no." But how can
groups and individuals make that decision in a more systematic and intelligent manner rather than simply by guesswork or
intuition?

Recognition that the social structure of a local area can
supplement, compete with, and even supplant the work of
professional social agencies is cause for renewed "outreach"
program innovation. Government and community change
agents must come to recognize that their goal is maximization
of community resources, not the creation of monolithic "service delivery systems." Moreover, it is important to view the
local neighborhood as providing a linkage between one system and another. Neighborhoods can in some instances provide an alternative to formal service systems. They may facilitate or subvert the utilization of such services as well.

The problem recognition and solution process is often
very much located within a set of networks or support sys-

tems. We are not trying to invent solutions to problems, rather we seek to learn how people themselves are inventing and discovering solutions.

There is a wide range of resources in the "neighborhood helping network." We feel that there are several layers of these systems. The formal, professional help-givers are at one point in that resource system. In between the formal professional helper and the lay-helper are other kinds of people. They may have joined together for a specific organizing purpose or may not see themselves as professionals.

We feel that it is very important to understand how these layers work. It is important, for example, to know if all of these layers are present in a given neighborhood or community. Are some very highly developed and utilized broadly? Are some virtually absent? How do these layers work together? How do they link together? How does the professional-helping system relate to the lay-helping system? How do the less specialized kinds of helpers learn about the needs of people? Do they relate to professionals and what is that relationship like? There are some very important questions about how this total set of resources is used by the individual.

This work looks at the social system of helping but from the perspective of the individual. The person with a problem or concern starts out on a path. We want to understand what sort of steps that person takes. What is the role of the neighborhood in that search? Are neighbors a first link in the help-seeking process?

One of the most serious consequences of urbanization and the forced migration of population groups—particularly minority groups—has been the destruction of the natural support system. The question which is a major policy concern for all of us is how do we preserve and strengthen these "natural" problem-solving systems?

We cannot really create these systems, but it is very possible that we can destroy them. All of us must recognize that strengthening communities, particularly local communities and neighborhoods, provides the capacity of people to mobilize and to deal with those new issues that they must confront. It is this *adaptive capacity* that is one of our society's most valuable human resources.

As we know from biological history, it is the continued capacity to adapt which represents the major means of survival. Overadjustment to a given problem results in danger to survival and to the disappearance of human cultures and values.

Neighborhoods and Social Change

What influence can the urban neighborhood have on the large-scale problems of blight, pollution, and economic fluctuation that characterizes the urban environment? In contrast to the view that neighborhoods are not significant in social change, we note three ways in which the neighborhood relates to social change processes and prospects:

1. Neighborhoods can provide a primary unit for governmental and private efforts at planned social intervention.

2. Given the high rate of built-in social change in a mass, industrial, bureaucratic society, local neighborhood primary groups may be able to respond to conditions of urban life more flexibly and effectively than formal organizations and welfare bureaucracies.

3. Neighborhood organizations can play a major role in clarifying and defining the solutions to urban problems by clearly differentiating problems with a local focus that are amenable to solution via local self-help and self-determination from those problems that clearly require wider bases of mobilization and collective action.

Thus, there are several unique functions the local neighborhood can play that no other social group seems to be as well equipped to do. Utilizing these special characteristics of the neighborhood will serve to place in proper perspective what is most likely to be successful versus distracting efforts to solve local area problems.

Often, during crises, the only operative resources that can react fast enough in a unique manner (based on complex histories of individual situations) and then recover to react again to a different problem are natural networks of helping relationships.

We question present diagnoses and preparations of communities for change (and disaster) with their heavy emphasis on professional action, technology, and central control. The implication is not for these extreme situations alone. Social networks derived from local informal relationships are uniquely and most capable of dealing with any problems that require low or modest technical knowledge. Where expert knowledge is nonexistent, the response must be complex, unique, and considerate of individual needs and situations, and where a rapid succession of different problems must be dealt with, social networks are the optimum approach.

What happens when individuals and whole neighborhoods are relocated in either urban-renewal projects or relocate themselves in new towns? There are inevitable problems of adjustment to a new social and physical environment. Normal patterns of problem solving (in both the professional and grass-roots systems and general social interaction) may be disrupted. If we had a thorough understanding of those processes and roles within a particular population's natural system of problem solving, we could improve the design of such new settlements in given settings, circumstances, and roles. At least we could minimize the grossly incompatible physical and social features of a new settlement and help limit the deleterious effects of the transition.

In many respects, programs of job training, medical care, and mental health are dependent on neighborhood ties and informal social norms for success or failure. Frequently the solutions people seek to problems are tied to their initial contacts with individuals with whom they speak and who, in turn, may suggest more formalized and institutionalized ways of handling problems. The initial solution of neighbors and friends may be effective and the individual may not have to seek a formal or professional service delivery system as the answer. Thus, as a filtering and a funneling process, local neighborhoods and informal groups derived from such settings become a basic way in which the more formal agencies of government and social welfare can more effectively plan sound programs.

Government and private industry have not utilized the local neighborhood concept in seeking to mobilize what may be the unique attributes of residents of given neighborhoods. Nor have they used the visibility of the local area as a way to facilitate or even to measure progress toward various social programs. Frequently, the successes of such programs in the area of employment, housing, social welfare, and mental health are lost in the vast complexity and anonymity of the total metropolitan community. It is important for social institutions to recognize that the issues of alienation and cynicism are often derived from the agencies' spreading of their services too thinly.

Utilizing the trial ground of the local neighborhood one can demonstrate that it is possible to reverse what appear to be the massive problems of the urban community and particularly those besetting inner-city areas. This is very much in the Saul Alinsky tradition of mobilization as a basis for later effective change. Such a process can be viewed as part of the function of local neighborhoods to clarify and differentiate problems in terms of their appropriate solution at various levels of the social structure of the community and of society. Thus, many local groups may be forced to use tactics and pursue goals which are clearly inappropriate for such a small-scale unit. By organizing and involving **people** at just one level, however, awareness of the need to locate particular problem solutions at other institutional levels can be generated. The issue is to recognize the sequential process, to view participation at the local level not as the *sine qua non* of community organization and cohesion but one avenue and perhaps but one step in a chain in levels of participation that the individual and the collective efforts of groups of individuals may pursue.

Neighborhood groups may come to realize that some problems are best approached through the abandonment of their localized efforts and the drawing upon a community-wide base of operations. By sensitizing groups to the cutting points of problem areas and creating a distinction between clearly local and clearly nonlocal issues, neighborhood groups provide important boundary-setting functions in the solution of urban problems. Much of the debate over the indigenous control of resources and decision making versus control by professional experts rests on the confusion of problems of technology with questions of value.

Professionals and community organization decision makers act on behalf of local groups presumably because of their superiority of knowledge. Yet neighborhood groups need to challenge the value premises of many such decisions. It is in this conflict and debate that the fuller delineation of solutions can emerge. Rather than coming to a final division of labor, this process of creative conflict between professionals and indigenous leaders becomes the basis for fundamental innovation in the urban community.

A Cautionary Note: The Selective Use of Neighborhoods in Social Intervention

Despite the foregoing discussion, the point should still be stressed that the neighborhood organization cannot provide many of the resources needed in contemporary industrial society. Much of the discontent and frustration with on-going neighborhood programs is based on the questioning of the assumption that organizations as such have power and should share in community decision making. Often they are effective only because of the linkage between middle-class residents through their peer and informal ties. Unless these patterns are associated with the neighborhood, such arenas are not neighborhood power bases. Creating organizations whose constituencies are not truly local only serves to deny the legitimate role of neighborhoods in community change. Channeling such energies into programs that provide social mobility for some residents of a neighborhood but leave others unaffected only serves to further discourage the urban resident caught in the middle and to make him more cynical about the efficacy of collective action.

To the extent that working-class and ghetto neighborhoods have an abundance of block clubs and voluntary associations, there is a knitting together of individuals whose primary commitment is to make an area respectable, or in some other fashion realize the goals presumably attained in middle-class neighborhoods. In the middle-class neighborhood, however, the main function of such groups tends to be social control—or the promulgation of special cultural patterns of child rearing or lifestyle.

To expect that modeling lower-class and ghetto areas after such self-selective social units will be successful is to misunderstand the needs and strengths of non-middle-class areas. Mutual aid, a sense of common problems, and the resources to marshal constant and effective influence against other community forces are likely to be lacking in part but seldom in toto. Assessment of these local organizational patterns is one of the major tasks of neighborhood organizers.

Neighborhoods can provide a way of coping with the pressures of change in the mass industrial society. This is true because of several unique aspects of neighborhoods as social institutions. These include: (1) the flexibility of small local groups and their ability to innovate more readily than larger institutions; (2) the direct contact as effective instruments of social control—neighborhood visibility providing for the enforcement of accepted values or for the creation of new ones; and (3) the rapid reaction to special problems that can only be present in an immediately accessible unit and which often cannot even be anticipated by larger institutions. We should not neglect the conservative side of neighborhood. For the individual the neighborhood can function as a buffer against the too rapid shocks of social change derived from our socioeconomic system.

How Strong Neighborhoods Function on Behalf of a Healthy Society

Totalitarian systems of the Twentieth Century have achieved success not on the ideological appeals they have put forth, but by their control over the neighborhood life of individuals. In fact, a good case can be made for saying the survival of democracy depends—in large measure—on the quality of political and social life within one's immediate neighborhood. These social worlds are very often the training ground of future political leaders as well as the crucible within which most people confront the often prodigious problems of our urban culture.

The neighborhood is a preservative institution in a value sense stemming from the need for structure and order in the life of the individual. In a larger sense, the richness and variety of neighborhood cultures and values provide concrete expression to the pluralistic composition of American society and its highly individualistic and self-deterministic value emphasis. The varieties of viable and effective neighborhoods we have discussed and identified in our research lend credence to that societal capacity.

The neighborhood in our view is a critical—although not the only—intersecting point between often isolated individuals and the mass society. This integrating role of the neighborhood is in actuality a dual one: first via the sense of belonging and community which many neighborhoods provide and, second, via the more utilitarian helping and problem-coping resources which residents in a given neighborhood possess.

Neighborhoods act in a subjective sense, as the anchor of an individual's community of place and in a more objective fashion by the actual use people make of their ties to neighbors and its potential for relating them into more distant networks. We believe building up the sense of local community in the neighborhood or the capacity of local contact to be effective in problem solving is not just a major agenda item for the neighborhood activist. The facilitation of neighborhood human resources should also serve as the foundation of an effective, enlightened, nonpaternalistic and meaningful national neighborhood policy. There is much room for exploration of such a policy direction in the planning and implementation of public programs at all levels—

municipal, state, and federal. Of necessity, we believe such efforts should be as direct as possible in terms of economic policy—reducing the threat to neighborhood life which particularly plagues inner-city areas—but otherwise indirect in terms of social engineering.

There can be no "creation" of community in a neighborhood where this is lacking. Economic strength will not alone achieve this goal. At the same time it is equally erroneous to provide local clinics, police-community outreach, or other human-service facilities when these are merely extensions of bureaucracy into the neighborhood. What must be recognized is the responsibility of social planners, policy elites, and local neighborhood activists to understand the distinct needs of a viable neighborhood in a collective sense. The role of a strong sense of *neighborhood* community is a desirable goal in and of itself—not just as a means of service delivery or reducing citizen alienation from bureaucracy.

While the major debate around neighborhood in the 1960s and early 1970s has been "local control," the agenda beyond would perhaps be more accurately summed up as the "enfranchisment of neighborhood."

Notes

CHAPTER 1

1. The legislation—known as Senate Bill 3554—was introduced on June 11, 1976, and reported out of the Senate Banking Committee on July 28, 1976. It is known as the "National Neighborhood Policy Act." Section 2 declares that "The Congress finds and declares that existing city neighborhoods are a national resource to be conserved and revitalized wherever possible and that public policy should promote that objective." For the report associated with the proposed legislation, see Calendar No. 988, 94th Congress, 2d Session. The bill passed the Senate, but the 94th Congress ended before the House of Representatives acted on the measure. A similar bill, at the time of this writing, is to be introduced in the 95th Congress.

2. Part of this ethic of the "good neighbor" includes defending that person even if you don't have any specific evidence on which to judge. When the former governor of Michigan, John Swainson, was indicted on several counts of perjury early in 1975, one story appeared under the headline, "Swainson's Neighbors Stunned." The story quoted nearby residents of the former governor and Supreme Court justice illustrating the disbelief in the charges and support for him: "I couldn't wish for a better neighbor.... He has done lots of nice things for me since my wife died.... I'm really hurt about this.... He always thought of other peoples' troubles, not his own.... If anyone says he took a bribe I know different. He's not that kind of person. Sure, he may have lied a little bit, but who doesn't? I do." *Ann Arbor News*, April 3, 1976.

3. Suzanne Keller, *The Urban Neighborhood: A Sociological Perspective* (New York: Random House, 1968), pp. 25–26.

4. Ethnographic observation report, June 18, 1975, "Helping Network Study." Unless otherwise indicated, quotations taken from neighbor observer field or taped debriefing sessions will be from this study funded by the National Institute of Mental Health.

5. Keller, *Urban Neighborhood*, p. 29.

6. Helena Z. Lopata, *Occupation: Housewife* (New York: Oxford University Press, 1971).

211

7. See Theodore Caplow and Robert Forman, "Neighborhood Interaction in a Homogeneous Community," *American Sociological Review* 15 (June 1950):357–66.

8. See Judith T. Shuval, "Class and Ethnic Correlates of Casual Neighboring," *American Sociological Review* 21, no. 4 (August 1956): 453–58.

9. See Shimon Spiro, "Effects of Neighborhood Characteristics on Participation in Voluntary Associations," (Ph.D. diss., University of Michigan, 1968).

10. See Scott Greer, "Urbanism Reconsidered: A Comparative Study of Local Areas in a Metropolis," *American Sociological Review* 21, no. 1, (February 1956):19–25.

11. David Morris and Karl Hess, *Neighborhood Power* (Boston: Beacon Press, 1975), p. 6.

12. Much of the research on neighborhoods by American and British sociologists is based on the processes of spatial sifting and sorting of populations that cause particular kinds of individuals and economic units to cluster together in metropolitan areas. The first empirical work on urban subareas was done by Robert Park and the "Chicago School" of urban sociology, beginning in the 1920s. By plotting indexes of correlations between the physical features of the city and rate of delinquency, mental disorder, and racial composition, they delimited "natural areas" of the urban community. The well-known concentric zonal hypothesis, which views urban growth as a process of widening spheres of specialized activity and population characteristics developing around a central downtown area or set of subcenters, illustrates this approach. By the mid-1950s, contemporary research approaches were applied to the spatially designated neighborhood concept in the work of Eshref Shevsky and Wendell Bell. Their analysis, published under the title *Social Area Analysis* (Stanford, California: Stanford University Press, 1955), is the culmination of the "ecological" approach. Ironically a more recent reanalysis of the patterns and functions of Chicago neighborhoods focuses on the social-psychological meaning of neighborhood. See Albert Hunter, *Symbolic Communities* (Chicago: The University of Chicago Press, 1974).

13. Keller, *Urban Neighborhood*, p. 1.

14. Morris and Hess, *Neighborhood Power*, p. 1.

15. Several studies have shown the relationship between the physical proximity and street pattern of a neighborhood and the facilitation and restriction these place on neighboring. See, for example, Leon Festinger "Architecture and Group Membership," *Journal of Social Issues*, no. 7 (1951):152–63.

16. See Donald I. Warren, *Black Neighborhoods: An Assessment of Community Power* (Ann Arbor: University of Michigan Press, 1975).

17. This example hints at the group basis of neighborhood life.

One of the participant observers in our own research found a situation where the basis of neighborhood was not simply the relationship of parents to the locale but exclusively the creation of that boundary and community life by the youth of a neighborhood: It seems that only children and teenagers in my neighborhood make real friendships. They approach each other with more ease and maintain the long-term relations easier. In fact, even the older generation's friends are mostly from school days, college, old neighborhood, or work; they are not neighbors. Teenagers know each other from high school or from church—here the networks overlap since children that go to the same church might not go to the same school. Children and teenagers who live on the same block or street maintain the most intense ties as neighbors too. They serve as a bridge for establishing good relationships between their parents. Mothers whose children play on the same street or go to the same school are most likely to start interacting regularly. Some meet at PTA meetings and discover that they live close to each other. According to one informant, garage sales that are organized jointly by several families are often initiated in fact by children of these families, not the adults, even though the latter might actually work on them. Helping Network Study Neighborhood Observation Report, May 1974.

18. One dominant theme in the sociological research on neighborhoods is the issue of whether such patterns of residential living are distinct phenomena in their own right or merely the indicators or expressions of social class, racial or ethnic composition, or other variables. Several researchers implied that local communities are simply expressions of social stratification patterns. For these analysts, social class, subcultures, and the neighborhood merge almost totally. For example, see the now classic work by Herbert Gans, *The Urban Villagers* (New York: The Free Press, 1962); Andrew Greeley's discussion of "Westwood" in *Why Can't They Be Like Us?* (New York: E. P. Dutton, 1971) also suggests the merging of class subculture and neighborhood. Two more theoretical discussions of the social class as cause or consequence are Dennis Wrong, "How Important is Social Class?" *Dissent:* Special Issue on the World of the Blue Collar Worker, 1972, pp. 278–285 and Stanislaw Ossowski, *Class Structure in the Social Consciousness* (New York: Macmillan, 1963). One study points to neighborhood not as merely the extension of social class but almost the reverse: class as the product of neighborhood. See George K. Hesslink, "The Functions of Neighborhood in Ecological Stratification," *Sociology and Social Research* 54, no. 4 (July 1970):441–59.

One way out of this dilemma of the "identification" problem, as it is often statistically expressed, is to treat neighborhoods in terms of a set of discrete dimensions, each of which can be independently measured and operationalized. In such an approach, some of the "functions" of the neighborhood serve to enforce social class norms and privileges or deprivations, and some can pertain to the relations of other social units and still others are unique to the nature of neighborhoods as social institutions.

19. Joseph B. Tamney, *Solidarity in a Slum* (New York: John Wiley & Sons, 1975), p. 28.

20. The work of Suzanne Keller, *Urban Neighborhood,* provides a full discussion of the neighboring role as does Helena Lopata, *Occupation: Housewife.* Keller (1968) provides a basic starting point for examining neighborhood by stressing the ambiguity of the role of neighbor ("the proximate stranger defending interests that are partly his own and partly those he shares with other neighbors"). What is more eloquently referred to as "physical proximity and spiritual uncertainty" can be separated from other types of primary group interactions. Unfortunately, past analysis of *neighboring* has equated the informal interchanges of physically proximate residents with the *neighborhood* as a social organization. As a result, we have a great deal of discussion about informal contact between persons who may reside next door to each other or who form a "micro-neighborhood" clustered within the larger areal unit. We instead define the sociability quotient as the probability of face-to-face contact in terms of extensivity—that is, the average across an entire neighborhood—on the average how many neighbors are contacted or known on a first-name basis. Caplow and Forman, "Neighborhood Interaction"; Terence Lee, "Urban Neighborhoods as a Socio-Spatial Schema," *Human Relations* 21, no. 3 (August 1968), pp. 241–67; and Leon Festinger, "Architecture and Group Membership," pp. 152–63, provide findings on these patterns.

On the qualitative aspects of neighboring see Peter H. Mann, "The Concept of Neighborliness," *American Journal of Sociology* 60, no. 2 (January 1954):163–68; James H. Williams, "Close Friendship Relations of Housewives Residing in an Urban Community," *Social Forces* 36 (May 1958):358–62; Robin M. Williams, Jr., "Friendship and Social Values in a Suburban Community: An Exploratory Study," *Pacific Sociological Review* 2 (Spring 1959):3–10; and Rudolf Heberle, "The Normative Element in Neighboring Relations," *Pacific Sociological Review* 3 (Spring 1960):3–11; Lee, "Urban Neighborhoods," pp. 241–67.

21. Ethnographic Field Notes, Helping Network Study, June 1974.

22. A number of studies have suggested that close friendship links exist between neighbor contacts and influence. One problem with this approach to neighboring influence is the assumption that contacts must be intimate and qualitatively significant. However, as Heberle, "Normative Element," indicates, there are normative patterns to neighboring and these determine social distance. Lee, "Ur-

ban Neighborhoods" points out that the mere volume of nodding acquaintances provides little basis for social influence.

Studies of the so-called "two-step flow of communication" are of significance here. A number of researchers have outlined the role of "opinion leaders"—people whose role in a community is to interpret the mass-media message for local primary groups. This process covers a wide range of topics from fashion to voting preferences. The nuclear neighborhood or extended neighborhood may be the field setting for such an influence process. This filtering role of local opinion leaders provides a mechanism both for integrating the individual into the large society where he might otherwise be isolated or to prevent the breakdown of local norms via the selective integration of values disseminated from the media or the larger community. See Paul F. Lazarsfeld, Bernard Berelson, and Hazel Gaudet, *The People's Choice* (New York: Columbia University Press, 1948); Robert K. Merton and A. S. Kitt, "Contributions to the Theory of Reference Group Behavior," in *Continuities in Social Research: Studies in the Scope and Method of "The American Soldier,"* ed. R. K. Merton and P. F. Lazarsfeld (Glencoe, Ill.: Free Press, 1950), pp. 87–89; Elihu Katz, "The Two-Step Flow of Communication: An Up-to-Date Report on an Hypothesis," *Public Opinion Quarterly* 21, no. 2 (Spring 1959):61–78.

A salient instance of the two-step process is found in the reactions of blacks and whites to the so-called "New Bethel Incident" in Detroit where two police officers were shot in early 1969. The study found that "what neighbors in the area have said" as one of four sources of information about the shooting incident ranked significantly higher among black versus white neighborhoods. Television and newspaper coverage was extensive and had a great impact on white attitudes about the police shoot-out. For blacks, primary group contacts with neighbors and friends was a mediating force, particularly in the case of individuals with more formal education. See Donald I. Warren, "Mass Media and Racial Crisis: A Study of the New Bethel Church Incident," *The Journal of Social Issues* 28, no. 1 (1972):111–32.

23. Ethnographic Field Report, Helping Network Study, June 1974.

24. Ethnographic Debriefing Session, Helping Network Study, June 1975.

25. Ethnographic Field Report, July 1974.

26. See Eugene Litwak and Ivan Szelenyi, "Primary Group Structures and Their Functions: Kin, Neighbors, and Friends," *American Sociological Review* 34 (August 1969):465–81.

27. William H. Form and Sigmund Nosow, *Community in Disaster* (New York: Harper and Row, 1958).

28. Ethnographic Field Report, Helping Network Study, May 1975.

29. Field Ethnographic Debriefing, July 1974.

30. Ethnographic Field Report, August 1974.

31. In a study of fatherless families, researchers found that mutual aid was extensive for employed mothers in fatherless families. Minor exchanges—borrowing or lending of groceries or small amounts of money, baby sitting, or shopping—were found to be frequent for both husbandless and married mothers in the survey population. Only 16 percent of the total sample did not report such exchange. Louis Kriesberg and Seymour S. Bellin, "Fatherless Families and Housing: A Study of Dependency, Final Report." (Washington, D.C.; U.S. Department of Health, Education and Welfare, 1965).

32. Donald I. Warren, "Neighborhood Structure and Riot Behavior in Detroit: Some Exploratory Findings," *Social Problems* 16 (Spring 1969):464–84.

33. Philip Fellin and Eugene Litwak, "Neighborhood Cohesion Under Conditions of Mobility," *American Sociological Review* 28, no. 3 (June 1963):364–76; and Fellin and Litwak, "The Neighborhood in Urban American Society," *Social Work* 13, no. 3 (July 1968):72–80.

34. Eugene Litwak, "Reference Group Theory, Bureaucratic Careers, and Neighborhood Primary Group Cohesion," *Sociometry* 23, (1960):72–84; and Litwak, "Voluntary Associations and Neighborhood Cohesion, *American Sociological Review* 26 (April 1961):258–71.

35. Ethnographic Field Report, July, 1974.

36. Peter H. Mann, "The Neighborhood," in *Neighborhood, City, and Metropolis,* ed. Robert Gutman and David Popenoe (New York: Random House, 1970), p. 581.

37. See for example Peter M. Blau, "Structural Effects," *American Sociological Review* 35 (May 1960):179–93; William H. Sewell and Michael J. Armer, "Neighborhood Context and College Plans, *American Sociological Review* 31, no. 2 (April 1966):159–68.

38. Albert J. Reiss and Albert L. Rhodes, "The Distribution of Juvenile Delinquency in the Social Class Structure," *American Sociological Review* 26, no. 5 (October 1961):720–32. See also Solomon Kobrin, "The Conflict of Values in Delinquent Areas," in *Social Perspectives on Behavior,* ed. Herman D. Stein and Richard A. Cloward (New York: The Free Press, 1958), pp. 498–505.

39. See Donald I. Warren, "Helping Networks, Neighborhood, and Community Patterns: Consequences for Personal Well Being," (Washington, D.C.: National Institute of Mental Health Final Report, Project 5R01–24982, August 1976).

40. John A. Clauson and Melvin L. Kohn, "The Ecological Approach in Social Psychiatry," *American Journal of Sociology* 60 (September 1954):140–51.

41. In the study in Detroit area settings it was found that in white

neighborhoods there tended to be a pattern for decorative additions to houses to be quite uniform on a given block. For instance, the gaslight lamppost, which was a frequent accessory in many middle-class or lower-middle-class homes, tended to be rather uniformly introduced on a given block where residents were white. When we examined this same pattern as it occurred in black ghetto neighborhoods, a different distribution was frequently found. In this case there tended to be a more disparate use of the external gaslight lamppost. In other words, black residents in relatively few instances had the same lamppost in terms of houses that were clustered near one another. Just as often these lampposts tended to be scattered on a fairly wide distribution throughout a given block rather than being uniformly clustered.

What do these differences suggest? In terms of the overall analysis, they seem to imply that for whites the external decoration of the home was a sign of conformity. In other words, the housing pattern of a given block tended to represent not just a membership group but also a reference group. By contrast, for black residents, the scattered pattern suggested that the lamppost was really a way not to conform but instead to differentiate oneself from neighbors. The reference group might be formed by those residents who would signal each other literally in terms of displaying the lamppost.

42. Firey, in studying land use in central Boston, concluded that "we find a symbol-sentiment relationship which has exerted a significant influence upon land use ... Further studies of this sort should clarify even further the true scope of sentiment and symbolism in urban spatial structure and dynamics." Walter Firey, "Sentiment and Symbolism as Ecological Variables," *American Sociological Review* 10 (April 1945):148.

Other research indicates that urban dwellers "frequently rely upon appearance rather than reputation: status may temporarily be appropriated by the 'correct' display and manipulations of symbols." William H. Form and Gregory P. Stone, "Urbanism, Anonymity, and Status Symbolism," *American Journal of Sociology* 62 (March 1957):512.

A similar point is made in a study of streetcorner life in which "exaggerated styles of personal interaction" are described. See Elliot Liebow, *Tally's Corner* (Boston: Little Brown and Company, 1967). See also Gerald Suttles, *The Social Order of the Slum* (Chicago: University of Chicago Press, 1968).

43. Form and Stone, "Urbanism."

44. Research in the last few years has focused on the nonspatial sociometric clusterings of friendship and "significant others" which has grown out of the work of cultural anthropologists. Thus, J. Clyde Mitchell defines a social network as "a specific set of linkages

among a defined set of persons, with the ... property that the characteristics of these linkages as a whole may be used to interpret the social behavior of the persons involved." J. Clyde Mitchell, "The Concept and Use of Social Networks," in *Social Networks in Urban Situations,* ed. J. Clyde Mitchell (Manchester: University of Manchester Press, 1969), p. 1.

A number of researchers have been using highly sophisticated computer techniques to describe the complex forms which sets of relationships may take. Several studies in England treat network analysis as the most useful approach to the analysis of community. Their importance has received a great deal of confirmation in studies in the North American context. For example see J. C. Mitchell and J. Boissevain, *Network Analysis* (The Hague: Mouton, 1973); Edward O. Laumann, *Bonds of Pluralism* (New York: John Wiley & Sons, 1973); Elizabeth Bott, *Family and Social Network,* 2d ed. (London: Tavistock Publishing, 1971); Jacqueline Scherer, *Contemporary Community: Sociological Illusion or Reality?* (London: Tavistock Publications, 1972); Paul Craven and Barry Wellman, "The Network City," *Sociological Inquiry* 43, no. 3 and 4 (1974):57–88.

45. Mark S. Granovetter, "The Strength of Weak Ties," *American Journal of Sociology* 78, no. 6 (May 1973):1360–79. Independently, other researchers have identified the value of "heterogeneity" of personal contacts and a notion of the strength "in weak ties." See William T. Liu and Robert W. Duff, "The Strength in Weak Ties," *Public Opinion Quarterly* 36, no. 3 (Fall 1972):361–66.

46. There is some hint of this idea in several recent research analyses of the "loss of community" and the role of neighborhood contact. See, for example, Albert Hunter, "The Loss of Community: An Empirical Test through Replication," *American Sociological Review* 40, no. 5 (October 1975):537–52. Claude Fischer argues that "relative freedom from spatial constraints available in the urban environment—that people within or without the neighborhood as they wish ... One can choose to be locally anonymous and yet still *not be isolated* because of the availability and ease of contacts outside the immediate area." Claude Fischer, "On Urban Alienations and Anomie: Powerlessness and Social Isolation," *American Sociological Review* 38 (June 1973):311–26; see also John D. Kasarda and Morris Janowitz, "Community Attachment in Mass Society," *American Sociological Review* 39, no. 3 (June 1974):328–39.

47. More directly on the issue of access to helping resources see Warren, "Helping Networks."

48. Peter Mann opens the question of neighborhood definition and then settles it by linking it to highly visible behaviors: "If Mr. Jones across the road goes off to work in his car each morning wearing his dark suit, white shirt and bowler hat, his actual job does

not really matter. But if he suddenly starts going out in greasy overalls, big boots, and a cloth cap, then it can matter because Mr. Jones is affecting the social status of the area in moving down the scale from an *apparent* nonmanual occupation to a manual one. The interesting point is that if he went to his work as a factory hand in a car and business suit, probably many people locally would be completely unaware of the dangerous situation that was at hand, since so much of the assessment is done through *visual evidence*" [emphasis added]. Mann "The Neighborhood," p. 538.

In this example and in his analysis, Mann has provided perhaps the one universal basis upon which definitions of neighborhood could be linked in some spatially critical way: *that is the neighborhood includes all those individuals and their behaviors that are visible in the normal course of one's residing in a given dwelling unit.* As we shall note in subsequent discussion, it is far from certain that the implications of neighborhood behavior in terms of social norms or other concepts having to do with the more common definition of "primary group" or "community" need characterize the essential nature of behaviors which are found among a group of people living in a given locale. Yet it is certainly plausible and perhaps especially desirable to include in one's definition of neighborhood the widest geographical area in which people travel or interact as a direct function of their living in a given dwelling. By so defining the household unit, it becomes the central point for observation. Some potential of the neighborhood as a totally *subjectively* meaningful social unit is thus given: It would include all of the spatial movements and their loci described by the population we have designated as neighbors. Ours is a more restrictive definition because we treat "pattern of social bonds" (which excludes much of the visible and spatial behavior of individuals living in a neighborhood). Neighborhood is not merely a perceptual reality but one involving the exchange of information, help, or social influence in behavior settings that are geographically fixed by the "walking distance" basis of neighborhood size. Neighborhood as the "behavior setting" is critical to our approach.

CHAPTER 2

1. Nathan Glazer, "The Limits of Social Policy," *Commentary* 52 (September 1971):3.

2. Ethnographic Field Report, Helping Network Study, September 1974.

3. Eugene Litwak and Henry J. Meyer, "The School and the Family: Linking Organizations and External Primary Groups," chapter

19 in *The Uses of Sociology,* ed. Paul F. Lazarsfeld, William H. Sewell and Harold L. Wilensky (New York: Basic Books, 1967), p. 529.

4. Ethnographic Field Report, Helping Network Study, July 1975.

5. Ethnographic Field Observer Notes, June 1975.

6. Detroit police advice includes the following: If at all possible, have someone keep an eye on the house and take in the mail. Stop deliveries. Have a neighbor clear the porch of handbills. Leave the shades and drapes in their normal positions. Preferably ask a neighbor to change them as you normally would. Make arrangements to have the lawn mowed in the summer or the snow cleared in winter. Uncared for property is a tip-off that no one's home. If you live in an apartment house, insist that it be equipped with good locks. The best is a dead-bolt interlocking lock with a pin tumbler. It is operated with a key rather than spring action and should extend into the door frame a half-inch or more. Purchase an automatic timer to turn lights on and off when you usually would. A constant light in a room that can't be looked into from the outside, such as a bathroom, is a good idea. It is also a good idea to leave one light on all night. Keep your garage locked. Lock your windows and equip them with a device that limits the height they can be raised. Restrict the opening to a maximum of four inches. Notify your local police department. Most have out-of-town lists, and patrol cars keep an eye on the houses.

Sgt. Don Nash of the Detroit Police Department said most burglaries occur during the day when no one is home. The best defense, he said, is to be in the house. "But if you're going away, get a neighbor or a relative to keep a close eye on it," he said. "A good neighbor can be a great asset." *Detroit Free Press,* July 14, 1976.

7. The tasks of the housesitter are very specialized and illustrate that much knowledge and discretion must be applied in carrying out the job. The housesitters are trained using a booklet printed on pink paper and offers such advice as "if the person likes repeat assignments don't leave anything behind except good will" and "put the usual size rubbish bag out front." Pat Hersey says that "there is a tremendous potential in this (housesitting professionals). But most people don't know how to find a housesitter. They don't put an ad in the paper saying 'Housesitter wanted' anymore. The answer is to have people do what I'm doing, with trained sitters who are bonded." She envisions a network of housesitting agencies spread throughout the country. She chaired the first meeting of a new organization she founded called the International Housesitters Association. *Detroit Free Press,* July 14, 1976.

8. Charles Kadushin, "The Friends and Supporters of Psychotherapy: On Social Circles in Urban Life," *American Sociologi-*

cal Review 31 (December 1966):6 and Kadushin, *Why People Go To Psychiatrists* (New York: Atherton Press, 1969).

9. Mark Granovetter, "Strength of Weak Ties."

10. Ethnographic Field Report, July 1975.

11. Ethnographic Debriefing Meeting, September 1975.

12. Ethnographic Field Report, October 1975.

13. Ethnographic Field Report, September 1975.

14. Ethnographic Field Report, August 1975.

15. Ethnographic Field Report, October 1975.

16. Often problems come in clusters and it is difficult to distinguish where to start first. Here's an extra case of the "multiproblem" neighborhood experienced by white residents and reported by our ethnographers:

> There is a somewhat local problem of age, older people v. younger people. There are specific neighborhood problems with the school. There is the hatred of the school, the hatred of the teachers. This kind of thing in the neighborhood really aggravates people—fears of what blacks moving in would do. They tell all kinds of really racist stories about all these drug people, and people who murder each other and get drunk. They go on and on with all these stories.
>
> And we asked about using the new park, too, since it was right there. One lady said that she didn't think any of her neighbors would send their kids over there any more. They did at one time, and she said a lot of it has to do with the cops coming back and telling stories. She goes over there with her son and his friends, and they're very rarely bothered. It's just this thing that's grown up around there.
>
> There was a newspaper boy who was killed, knifed to death by blacks, a couple of months ago. That was in another neighborhood, but it was only several blocks away from this neighborhood. Obviously this didn't help calm people's fears.

CHAPTER 3

1. David Horton Smith, "The Importance of Formal Voluntary Organizations for Society," *Sociology and Social Research* 50 (July 1966):486; see also Smith, "A Psychological Model of Individual Participation in Formal Voluntary Associations," *American Journal of Sociology* 73 (September 1967):235–44.

2. Ethnographic Debriefing Meeting, September 1975.

3. Ethnographic Report, Helping Network Study, August 1975.

4. Ethnographic Field Report, October 1975.

5. Ethnographic Field Report, Helping Network Study, July 1974.

6. A good description of how this comes about is the following: There are ways in which democratic decision-making and full participation by the rank and file in a neighborhood can be undercut. Early in the formation of a group a decision must be made as to structure, and while democratic structure does not guarantee democracy, it does help. A decision must also be made on how decisions are to be taken: by parliamentary system or by consensus (the Quaker "sense of the meeting") methods. Both have advantages, and both have disadvantages. Consensus tends to work best when the members of the group have basic agreement on philosophy, while the parliamentary system tends to guarantee representation to organized minorities and recognizes the importance of caucuses. Both systems can be manipulated by persons with the best intentions, not to speak of those with less than the highest moral outlook.

Several kinds of conditions, (aside from outside manipulation) help to undermine democracy or help make manipulation possible. Wearing the group out with late and boring meetings or holding the group until most members have gone leaves the way open for a well-organized minority to railroad proposals through. Having present officers appoint or elect other officer should generally be regarded with suspicion. Nominating committees for officers, rather than nominations from the floor, is another technique for keeping decision-making within a small group. Most important of all is the development of informal person-to-person relationships: shortcuts, doing favors, and the praiseworthy but misdirected desire to want to avoid mistakes—hence letting "experts" do all the jobs. This tends to happen particularly in the midst of crises and emergencies when "we can't afford to make mistakes" and can't take a chance on letting an untrained person do a job and learn at the risk of having him make mistakes. Martin Oppenheimer and George Lakey, *A Manual for Direct Action* (Chicago: Quadrangle Books, 1964), p. 44.

7. This discussion is based on Donald I. Warren, *Black Neighborhoods,* chapter 5, pp. 70–96.

8. Ethnographic Observation Report, June 1974.

9. These definitions and concepts are derived from the work of several researchers. Most importantly, there is the work of Freed Bales, *Interaction Process Analysis: A Method for the Study of Small Groups* (Reading, Mass: Addison-Wesley, 1950); Freed Bales, "Task and Social Roles in Problem Solving Groups," in *Readings in Social Psychology,* ed. Eleanor Maccoby, T. M. Newcomb and E. L. Hartley, 3d ed. (New York: Holt, Rinehart and Winston, 1958); R. F. Bales and P. E. Slater, "Role Differentiation in Small Decision Making Groups," in

Family, Socialization and Interaction Process, ed. Talcott Parsons and R. Freed Bales (Glencoe: The Free Press, 1955).

10. Robert Michels, *Political Parties: A Sociological Study of the Oligarchical Tendencies of Modern Democracy* (New York: The Free Press, 1962).

11. In defining the nature of leadership, social scientists have used at various times three basic approaches. The first of these has been to ask those individuals in a particular population who were the persons who played important roles in making decisions. A second approach is to look at the various organizations and institutions within a group and to identify those persons with a formal position at the head of such organizations. A third approach is to trace out particular issues that are important to a community and look at the individuals who play a role in the process of arriving at a decision. A somewhat classic instance of the first of these approaches is the work by Floyd Hunter, entitled *Community Power Structure* (Chapel Hill: University of North Carolina Press, 1953). He relies on what is usually described as the "reputational" approach to power.

12 In our studies we have identified those persons whose respect and reputation were visible enough so that they could form a group or a strata within the neighborhood and who were identified as leaders when people were asked. We used a "snowball" sample approach to identify neighborhood activists. This involved obtaining relatively exact information about each activist. Such a procedure of contacting "nominated" activists is analogous to the study of top leadership presented by Floyd Hunter in which a reputational approach is central: How many people can name a "leader" and who gets more than one nomination and who is nominated by other "leaders"? Once armed with "activist lists" we asked them directed questions about their roles.

13. These findings are based on a major survey of twenty-eight neighborhoods supported by the National Institute of Mental Health and conducted between 1969 and 1970 in the city of Detroit and two adjacent communities. A total of 196 individuals were identified as reputational activists by respondents we interviewed in the various neighborhoods.

The prior published reports and analysis papers regarding our findings on neighborhood activists include chapters 25 through 27 in Donald I. Warren, *Race and Community Structure,* U.S. Department of Health, Education and Welfare, Final Report, Project USPHS 1R01 MH 16403, December 31, 1971; Donald I. Warren, *Black Neighborhoods,* chapter 6; and Rachelle B. Warren and Donald I. Warren, "Neighborhood Activists: Description, Prescription and Proscription," paper delivered at the Annual Meeting of the Society for the Study of Social Problems, San Francisco, California, August 1975.

CHAPTER 4

1. Morris and Hess, *Neighborhood Power*, recognize this problem and attempt in their chapter entitled, "Developing Neighborhood Awareness: The First Institutions" to provide some overview. Another useful source is Milton Kotler *Neighborhood Government: The Local Foundations of Political Life* (Indianapolis, Ind.: Bobbs-Merrill, 1960). Irving A. Spergel in his *Community Problem Solving: The Delinquency Example* (Chicago: The University of Chicago Press, 1969), provides a solid focus on different tactics and local community organizer roles. Robert Perlman and Arnold Gurin, *Community Organization and Social Planning* (New York: John Wiley and Sons, 1972), devote some time to a discussion of the use of neighborhood voluntary associations as action strategies. Arthur Hillman and Frank Seever, *Making Democracy Work* (New York: National Federation of Settlements and Neighborhood Centers, 1968), provide an informative effort to conceptualize the goals, strategies, and participation efforts of neighborhood organizations.

2. Lee Rainwater, "Neighborhood Action and Lower Class Life Style" in *Neighborhood Organization for Community Action*, ed. John B Turner (New York: National Association of Social Work, 1968); Hillman and Seever, *Making Democracy Work;* Si Kahn, *How People Get Power* (New York: McGraw-Hill, 1970).

3. See for example Charles F. Grosser, "Staff Role in Neighborhood Organization," in *Neighborhood Organization for Community Action*, ed. J. B. Turner, pp. 133–59; Irving A. Spergal, *Community Problem Solving*, develops a taxonomy of different local community organizer role emphases. For a stimulating effort to conceptualize the way the local organizer can relate to formal organizations see Eugene Litwak, Earl Shiroi, Libby Zimmerman, and Jessie Bernstein, "Community Participation in Bureaucratic Organizations: Principles and Strategies" *Interchange* 1 (1970):44–60. The strategies and pitfalls of local organizer roles is discussed in Edmund M. Burke, "Citizen Participation Strategies," *Journal of the American Institute of Planners*, 34, no. 5 (September 1968):287, 294. The foregoing article as well as several other efforts to explore the local organizer's behavior is found in Ralph M. Kramer and Harry Specht, *Readings in Community Organization Practice*, 2d ed. (Englewood Cliffs, N.J.: Prentice Hall, 1974).

4. A useful recent text in the field is that of Joan L. Ecklein and Armand A. Lauffer, *Community Organizers and Social Planners*, chapter on "Organizing at the Neighborhood Level" (New York: John Wiley and Sons, 1972).

5. Morris and Hess, *Neighborhood Power*, chapter 8, pp. 144–58.

6. Floyd Hunter, *Community Power Structure*.

7. C. Wright Mills, *The Power Elite* (New York: Oxford University Press, 1956).

8. Si Kahn, *How People Get Power,* chapter 3, pp. 21–37.

9. Kahn argues that "where organizers and power structures have tried to con each other, the power structure has very often been the winner usually because the organizer failed to believe that the power structure could use the same tactics he was using and use them as well or better. A good organizer always assumes that the other side is using all the tactics that he is and using them at least as well." *How People Get Power,* p. 29.

10. Burke, "Citizen Participation Strategies," p. 202.

11. See Donald I. Warren, *Black Neighborhoods,* pp. 65–69 passim.

12. Litwak and Meyer, "The School and the Family."

13. These Strategies are discussed in Litwak, Shiroi, et al., "Community Participation in Bureaucratic Organizations."

14. See ibid., pp. 465–81.

15. The theme of interrelatedness of neighborhoods and local communities with a larger functionally bound system of community is found in much of the work of Roland Warren. See his *Perspectives on the American Community* (Chicago: Rand McNally, 1973) and *The Community in America,* p. 242.

16. Charles Grosser, "Staff Role," p. 135.

CHAPTER 5

1. See for example Reiss and Rhodes, "Juvenile Delinquency"; Kobrin, "Conflict of Values"; and Alan B. Wilson, "Residential Segregation of Social Classes and Aspirations of High School Boys," *American Sociological Review* 24 (December 1959):836–45.

2. An important study on the impact of urban renewal in terms of neighborhood mobilization is Clarence J. Davies, *Neighborhood Groups and Urban Renewal* (New York: Columbia University Press, 1966).

3. For a discussion from the perspective of the Federal "establishment" see *U.S. President's Task Force on Model Cities: A Step Towards the New Federalism,* (Washington, D.C.: Government Printing Office, 1970).

4. These efforts are based on revenue sharing and block grants by the federal Government to cities.

5. The first two factors have been discussed in chapter 1 under neighborhood as a reference group and the sociability quotient. Each of the three dimensions have been alluded to or directly measured in various studies and research approaches in both the sociology and community organization literatures. On interaction see in particular Suzanne Keller, *Urban Neighborhood;* Wendell Bell and

Marion D. Boat, "Urban Neighborhoods and Informal Social Relations," *American Journal of Sociology* 62 (July 1957):391–98; Caplow
and Forman, "Neighborhood Interaction"; Lee, "Urban Neighborhood"; Mann, "Neighborliness"; Mann, "The Neighborhood."

In regard to the second social structural dimension—identity—see
Mann, "The Neighborhood." He discusses the idea of "things in
common" which we have used to measure neighborhood patterns.
Of particular interest in more recent work is the analysis by Albert
Hunter, *Symbolic Communities.* Gerald Suttles discusses the critical
role of "symbolic interaction" in his *Social Construction of Communities*
(Chicago: University of Chicago Press, 1972).

The linkage dimension is discussed extensively by Roland Warren
in his major overview *The Community in America,* 2d ed. (Chicago:
Rand McNally, 1972). Fellin and Litwak, "Neighborhood Cohesion,"
also describe neighborhood ties to the larger community via the
mobility and voluntary-association memberships of local residents.
On the lack of linkage see Herbert Gans, *Urban Villagers;* Davies,
Neighborhood Groups. The discussion of the need to view community
in terms of not just one dimension but several is developed by Marcia
P. Effrat, "Approaches to Community: Conflicts and Complemen-
taries," *Sociological Inquiry* 43, no. 3 and 4 (1974):1–30.

6. The first use of the typology is found in Donald I. Warren,
"Neighborhood Structure and Riot Behavior in Detroit: Some Ex-
ploratory Findings," *Social Problems* 16 (Spring, 1969):464–84. Also
D. I. Warren, *Black Neighborhoods,* op. cit., typology in chapter 4, pp.
61–65. Use of the typology to measure both patterns of energy con-
servation and response to life crises events in D. I. Warren and David
L. Clifford, "Local Neighborhood Social Structure and Response to
the Energy Crisis of 1973–1974," paper read at the 69th Annual
Meeting of the American Sociological Association, San Francisco,
California, August 1975; and Forrest W. Graves, Jr., "Psychosomatic
Symptoms Associated with Vital Life Crises: An Exploratory
Analysis of Self-Perceived Neighborhood Contexts" (Master's thesis,
Eastern Michigan University, 1975).

Use of the neighborhood typology was linked to actual household
energy use patterns. See Donald I. Warren, *A Pilot Study Relating
Actual Household Natural Gas Usage to Social Organization Patterns of
Neighborhoods* (Ann Arbor: Institute of Labor and Industrial Rela-
tions, January 1976). Extensive utilization of the typology is found in
the report on problem solving and mental well being reported in D.
I. Warren, "Helping Networks, Neighborhood and Community
Patterns: Consequences for Personal Well-Being."

7. These include a situation of high identity, low interaction, and
high linkage and low identity, high interaction, and low linkage. The
first of these was found in three out of fifty-nine neighborhoods in

the Helping Network Study and the second type occurred twice, both in the same small community. In the former instance the neighborhood type can be seen as very temporary given that the high identity will not remain unless it is rather quickly followed by the development of more social contact. In the latter instance high interaction would be seen to lead in the short run to more identity. Thus, we expect that the situation of a neighborhood with linkages and local identity would gain in interaction and become an integral neighborhood, while the neighborhood lacking identity would become parochial given the lack of linkages but the high level of interaction.

Since over a five-year period fifteen of twenty-seven neighborhoods in which a typing was made for the same area at both points in time had changed types, it is clear that the social organization of a neighborhood is very dynamic—even in short time intervals. For the two forms we have discussed their transformation to integral or parochial or to one of the other major types of neighborhoods would be expected to occur within a five-year period. More research is needed to ascertain how neighborhood social organization changes and which dimensions are most "volatile." Our own evidence indicates that identity is the least stable factor and interaction is the most—with linkage patterns changing almost as quickly as identity. We need more follow-up data from our present neighborhood samples to validate and extend the tentative findings on neighborhood social organization change.

8. The quotes are taken from personal interviews with the respondents in the studies conducted in 1969 and 1974. They are the verbatim answers to the questions noted at the beginning of each sequence. They are designated in each case by the sex and age of the individual only. Additional sets of interview quotes will be used at several points in this chapter.

9. Ethnographic Field Report, Helping Network Study, July 1974.

10. Ethnographic Field Report, Helping Network Study, June 1975.

11. Community Ethnographic Report, Helping Network Study, June 1974.

12. Ethnographic Debriefing Report, May 1975.

13. Ethnographic Field Report, Helping Network Study, August 1974.

14. Ethnographic Field Report, Helping Network Study, October 1975.

15. Ethnographic Field Report, Helping Network Study, September 1975.

16. See Roland Warren, *Studying Your Community*.

17. Several studies of the role of density in neighborhood satisfaction as well as mental outlook have been carried out. On the first point see Lee, "Urban Neighborhood"; Festinger, "Architecture and Group Membership." In particular see P. John Zeisel, *Sociology and Architecture* (New York: Russell Sage Foundation, 1975).

18. See for example Bennett M. Berger, *Working Class Suburb* (Berkeley: University of California Press, 1968); Sylvia Fava, "Suburbanism as a Way of Life," *American Sociological Review* 21, no. 1 (February 1956): 34–37 and her more recent article "Beyond Suburbia," *Annals of the American Academy of Political and Social Science* 422 (November 1975):10–24.

19. Author's Ethnographic Field Notes, June 1974.

20. Ethnographic Field Report, June 1974.

21. Ethnographic Field Notes, July 1974.

22. Ethnographic Field Report, August 1974.

CHAPTER 6

1. Recently several colleagues at the University of Michigan studied the communication patterns in two medium-sized midwestern communities. We included questions in their study which allow a systematic look at how neighborhoods affect the flow of information in our society. Essentially we grouped people by their perceived neighborhood setting using the basic six types of settings. We then looked at how much time they spent watching television and reading newspapers, how many people in local government or business or key community people they knew, how often they talked with friends and neighbors about the things they read or watched on TV, and how much a neighbor was a reliable source for interpreting events in the world around them.

The discussion in this chapter is based on an analysis of 440 respondents in Toledo, Ohio, and Flint, Michigan. See Donald I. Warren and John P. Robinson, "Information and Neighborhood Context: Evidence from a Two City Sample" (unpublished paper, The University of Michigan, January, 1975).

2. Whether it is the "war of the worlds" phenomena or—as we found in a related study—the polarization of views of a racially defined police issue, the anomic-neighborhood context can be seen as the triggering mechanism for such reactions. See Donald I. Warren "Mass Media and Racial Crisis: A Study of the New Bethel Church Incident," *The Journal of Social Issues* 28, no. 1, pp. 111–32.

3. The patterns and data reported are derived from interviews with neighborhood activists as described in chapter 4.

4. The full list is as follows: church-connected groups, labor unions, parent-teacher organizations, professional associations, so-

cial clubs, ethnic or nationality groups, neighborhood-improvement associations, block clubs, fraternal organizations, social-action groups, civic groups, charitable organizations, youth groups, veterans organizations, senior-citizens groups, study and cultural groups, civil-rights groups, and political-party organizations. See D. I. Warren, *Black Neighborhoods*, p. 159.

CHAPTER 7

1. This portion of the chapter is based on an article which appeared in *Psychology Today*. Donald I. and Rachelle B. Warren, "Six kinds of Neighborhoods," *Psychology Today* 9, no. 1 (June 1975):74–79.

CHAPTER 8

1. As part of the National Institute of Mental health study "Helping Networks in the Urban Community" (3 R01-MH-24982), a total of fifty-nine elementary school districts in Detroit and ten surrounding communities composed an extensive sample in which both household interviews and neighborhood observation data were gathered. In the first instance a series of interview questions were aggregated for the thirty-five to forty households which served to represent their neighborhood. By these means each of the fifty-nine neighborhoods was classified within the typology we have discussed. In addition, a total of twenty-five neighborhoods were classified in a separate manner by the two-person neighborhood ethnographic teams. After comparing the classifications of the interviews and the observations there were several instances of dissimilarity. While by formal interview several neighborhoods were typed as anomic, the observation approach tended to find more activity and "strength" to the neighborhood. Thus, fewer anomic types emerged using this particular observation methodology.

A discussion of how the particular method of classifying neighborhoods is closely intertwined with the kind of neighborhood being studied is contained in an unpublished paper entitled "The Measurement of Local Community Patterns: The Use of Multiple Investigative Strategies" by Donald I. Warren (University of Michigan, August, 1975). Basic parts of this discussion include the initial method used to classify and the types of neighborhood requiring several techniques to insure a high validity to the typing. This discussion is an expression of the close link between theory and method in social science.

2. For several valuable discussions on the debate over different research techniques see: John C. Ball, "The Reliability and Validity of Interview Data Obtained from 59 Narcotic Drug Addicts," *American Journal of Sociology* 72 (May 1967):650–54; Donald T. Campbell, "The Informant in Quantitative Research," *American Journal of Sociology* 60 (1955):339–42; George J. McCall, and J. L. Simmons (ed.), *Issues in Participant Observation.* (Reading, Massachusetts: Addism-Wesley 1969); Sam D. Sieber, "The Integration of Fieldwork and Survey," *American Journal of Sociology* 78 (May 1973):1335–59; Martin Trow, "Comment on 'Participant Observation and Interviewing: A Comparison'" *Human Organizations* 16, no. 3 (1957):33–35; Arthur J. Vidich, and Gilbert Shapiro, "A Comparison of Participant Observation and Survey Data," *American Sociological Review* 20 (1955):28–33; William F. Whyte, *Streetcorner Society* (Chicago: University of Chicago Press, 1955); and Morris Zelditch, "Some Methodological Problems of Field Studies," *American Journal of Sociology* 67 (1962):566–76.

3. This portion of the chapter is based on an unpublished paper and field work guide by Rachelle B. Warren entitled "The 'Ethos' of Neighborhood Ethnography," written with the assistance of Louise Berndt, University of Michigan, August 1974.

CHAPTER 9

1. An effort to define the *ought* of local neighborhoods and the potential which needs development is to be found in Roland Warren's essay, "The Good Community." In his analysis, Warren distinguishes an approach to local community in terms of concrete collectivities versus other approaches which he labels the "new ecology." Several dimensions of local community are discussed, all of which highlight the issues confronting those who would engage in a debate about "good" neighborhoods: primary group relations, autonomy, viability, power distribution, participation, degree of commitment, degree of heterogeneity, extent of neighborhood control, and the extent of conflict. Each dimension is seen as a value to be weighed in terms of the desired maximum or minimum level of what constitutes the good community. The result is a balancing process between the multiple attributes composing such a model and the interplay and political forces shaping these options.

Far less hindered by the complexity and competition between desired attributes of the good neighborhood is the discussion by David Morris and Karl Hess, *Neighborhood Power: The New Localism.* Eschewing the limitations and skepticism of empirical researchers, they see neighborhoods as the "fundamental unit of democracy."

They strongly advocate building economically and politically strong neighborhoods. Such visions ignore the dangers of protectionism and parochialism; these are swept aside in favor of viewing neighborhoods as analogous to underdeveloped societies whose resources and human potential can and should be harnessed in the interests of their residents. Prescriptions for successful organization and development of neighborhoods are presented as techniques to be emulated on a wide scale.

2. Saul Alinsky and the methods of direct, conflict-oriented approaches to community organization are, of course, an important chapter in the development of social action for neighborhoods. His basic philosphy is discussed in *Reveille for Radicals* (Chicago: The University of Chicago Press, 1945). A more specific introduction to his style and its application is found in the article "Community Analysis and Organization," *American Journal of Sociology* 46 (1941):797–808. See also Alinsky's "Citizen Participation and Community Organization in Planning and Urban Renewal," Mimeographed. Chicago: Industrial Areas Foundation, January, 1962.

Index